PORTUGAL

PORTUGAL

YVES BOTTINEAU

With
168 photographs by Yan

THE STUDIO PUBLICATIONS INC.
in association with
THOMAS Y. CROWELL COMPANY
NEW YORK

TRANSLATED FROM THE FRENCH BY

ERIC EARNSHAW SMITH

All rights reserved 1957
First published in France by B. Arthaud Grenoble
Photogravure plates printed by Ets Braun et Cie Mulhouse
Text printed in Great Britain by Jarrold & Sons Ltd Norwich

Contents

	Introduction	11
I	Oporto and the Northern Districts	41
II	Coimbra and its Surroundings	82
III	From Tomar to Nazaré	121
IV	Lisbon and the Banks of the Tagus	162
V	Evora and the Alentejo	221
VI	The Algarve	245
	Conclusion	265
	The Kings and Queens of Portugal	272
	Index	273

List of Plates

1. Fisherman's wife
2. The Tagus
3. Lisbon. Gardens of the Palacio Fronteira
4. Near Nazaré
5. Noria
6. On the Mondego
7. Typical scenes of the life . . .
8. . . . in the villages of the west coast
9. Church of Lourinhã. St John at Patmos
10. Museum of Viseu. Vasco Fernandes. Detail from The Calvary
11. Coimbra. Retable of the High Altar of the Cathedral
12. Landscape in Trás-os-Montes
13. Bragance
14. Mirandela
15–16. Near Miranda do Douro
17. Harvest on the Chaves road
18. Guimarães
19. Braga. The Bom Jesus do Monte
20–22. Braga. The Cathedral. Nossa Senhora da Leite and Ex-Voto
23–25. Braga. The Festival of St John
26. Viana do Castelo. Portal of the parish church
27. Procession in Viana do Castelo
28. Around Ponte do Lima
29. Fish drying in the sun
30. Oporto
31. Oporto. The Dom Luis I Bridge
32. At Oporto
33–34. The old and new Oporto

List of Plates

35	Oporto. Carmelite Church
36	Oporto. The São Sebastião Fountain
37	On the Douro
38	Wine harvesting near Vila Nova de Familição
39	Near Barcelos
40	Guarda. The Cathedral terrace
41	Castelo-Branco. Gardens of the old Episcopal Palace
42	Viseu. The Misericordia
43	Near Aveiro
44–46	Aveiro. Moliceiros on the Ria
47	Coimbra. View on to the Cathedral
48	Coimbra. Patio of the Machado de Castro Museum
49	Coimbra. The new University seen from the Porta Ferrea
50	Coimbra. The Via Latina
51	Coimbra. Ceiling of the Library of the University
52	Coimbra. The Monastery of Santa Cruz. Pulpit of Nicholas Chanterène
53	Coimbra. Towards the Cathedral
54	Coimbra. Door of the Palacio Sub-Ripas
55	Coimbra. The Machado de Castro Museum. The Black Christ
56	Coimbra. The old Santa Clara Convent
57–59	Coimbra. Festival of the Rainha Santa
60	Bussaco. Staircase of the Fonte Fria
61	In Beira
62	Tomar. The Monastery of Christ
63–66	Tomar. The Monastery of Christ. Details
67	Tomar. The Monastery of Christ. Rotunda of the Church of the Templars
68	Tomar. The Monastery of Christ. St Jerome
69–72	Pilgrims at Fatima
73	Leiria seen from the Castle
74	The Batalha Monastery. The Unfinished Chapels
75	The Batalha Monastery
76–77	The Batalha Monastery. Royal Cloister

78–79 The Batalha Monastery. The Unfinished Chapels. Portal and vaulting of Mateus Fernandes
80 Alcobaça. The Santa Maria Monastery. Detail of Dom Pedro's Tomb
81 Alcobaça. The Santa Maria Monastery. Mausoleum of Ines de Castro and Dom Pedro I
82 Alcobaça. The Santa Maria Monastery. The Monks' Refectory
83–93 Fishers and women of Nazaré
94 Vila Franca di Xira. The Maréchal Carmona Bridge
95 Lisbon from the Tagus
96 Lisbon. Varinas
97 Lisbon. Casa dos Bicos
98 Lisbon. Praça dos Restauradores
99 Lisbon. The Cathedral
100 Lisbon. Carmelite Church
101 Lisbon. The St George Castle
102 Lisbon. A street in the Alfama
103–104 Lisbon. In the Alfama
105 Lisbon. The harbour
106 Lisbon. The Belem Tower
107–108 Details from the Belem Tower
109 Lisbon. The Monastery of the Hieronymites
110 Lisbon. The Monastery of the Hieronymites. Detail from the façade
111 Lisbon. Cloister of the Hieronymites Monastery
112 The Hieronymites Monastery. Christ of the Tribune
113 Lisbon. Museum of Ancient Art. Portrait of the King Dom Sebastião
114 Lisbon. Museum of Ancient Art. Portrait of Isabel de Moura
115–119 Lisbon. Museum of Ancient Art. Retable by Nuno Gonçalves
116 Retable by Nuno Gonçalves. Knight with spear
117 Retable by Nuno Gonçalves. Side-panel showing the fishermen. Detail
118 Retable by Nuno Gonçalves. Fishermen
119 Retable by Nuno Gonçalves. St Vincent

List of Plates

- 120 *Azulejos* in the São Vicente de Fora Church
- 121 The park of Queluz Castle
- 122 Sintra. The Pena Castle
- 123–124 At Sesimbra
- 125 Setubal
- 126 The Campinos of the Ribatejo
- 127–134 Bull-fighting
- 135 View of Evora
- 136 Evora. The Cathedral. The Lantern Tower
- 137 Evora. The Cathedral. The Triforium
- 138 Evora. The Cathedral Porch. Apostles
- 139 Evora. The Cathedral Porch. St Peter
- 140 Evora. View of the Temple of Diana
- 141 Evora. The São Francisco Convent. The Casa dos Ossos
- 142 At Elvas
- 143 Vila Viçosa. Gate of Knots
- 144 A house in the Alentejo
- 145 At Portalegre
- 146–147 In Alentejo
- 148–149 Beja. Rooms in the Conceição Convent, now the local museum
- 150 Towards Beja
- 151 Lagos
- 152 In the Serra de Monchique
- 153 Village in Algarve
- 154–157 Collecting the cork in the Serra de Monchique
- 158 Cabo de Sagres
- 159 Praia da Rocha
- 160 Sagres. The water-seller
- 161 Woman of Tavira
- 162–163 Tunny fishing
- 164 A Portuguese type
- 165 Procession
- 166–167 Feasts
- 168 At Praia de Vieira

Introduction

SITUATED on the south-west flank of Europe and occupying, with an area of about 34,000 square miles, the greater part of the western coast of the Iberian peninsula, Portugal may be briefly described as the stairway down which the Meseta slopes to the sea. This geographical situation and configuration account for many of the characteristics which so sharply differentiate the country from Spain, on whose flank Portugal forms a rectangle about 360 miles in length and 120 in width. The frontier between the two countries extends for about 750 miles, the coastline for only 520; but it is the sea which has made Portugal what she is—an Atlantic nation, Latin in culture, with powerful Muslim influences. The fact is that mountains and desert lands frequently act as a barrier, whereas the sea unites. The only way in which the young Portuguese nation could establish itself next door to the neighbouring Castile was by discovering and asserting its true destiny, and this did not lie to the east. There the way was barred by Spain, from whose domination Portugal was fortunate to escape. There remained the sea. From the sea came the kindly rains to water and fertilize the soil. From the sea the inhabitants acquired a love of independence and a thirst for adventure which led them to magnificent discoveries, to fame and wealth, and to the foundation of an empire thanks to which Portugal is still today a great country.

The slope of the Meseta to the sea shows wide divergences between north and south. In the north the central granitic plateau falls sheer into the sea: the mountain chains form a tangled mass, like those in neighbouring Galicia, the frontier being marked only by the river Minho. In the south, on the other hand, only a few advanced spurs reach as far as the sea. Thus to the west we find a certain number of Tertiary formations through which flow, in particular, the rivers Tagus and Sado. The river-deposits have choked up the coasts, which provide long sandy stretches between cape and cape, sometimes consisting of pine tracts. The *ria*, or estuary of Aveiro at the mouth of the river Vouga, has nothing but the name in common with the *rias* of Galicia: it is actually a lagoon cut up into canals and gradually encroached upon by the dry land. In the extreme south, the province of Algarve, largely consisting of carboniferous strata projected from the Serra Morena, presents a more rugged surface than the centre of the country. The coast, west of Santa Maria, is rocky and indented by the sea; whereas to the east there is a succession of small alluvial river-plains.

Apart from the Algarve, the most mountainous regions lie north of a line running from the north-east corner of the frontier to Cape Roca near Lisbon. In the north, the mountains of Galicia and Portugal are spread out like a fan. But the Meseta rises in height as it thrusts westwards, causing the valley of the Douro to become more steeply embanked. Where the valley is sufficiently remote from the cooling effect of the sea, a natural hothouse is produced for the cultivation of the famous vines.

North of the Douro the principal mountain ranges are the Nogueira (4,324 feet) and the Marão (4,642 feet). In the south the altitudes are decidedly lower, except in the Beira provinces, where the Serra da Estrêla and its extension the Serra da Lousa reach an altitude of 6,535 feet, the highest in Portugal. North of the Tagus there is a small group of mountains which includes, at its south-western corner near Lisbon, the Serra da Sintra. The Serra de Arrabida, which terminates in Cape Espichel and gives its shape to the Setubal peninsula, is of comparatively recent formation.

The climate of Portugal conforms to the Mediterranean type, extremes of temperature being diminished by the country's geographical situation in the south of Europe, by the low altitude and the proximity of the sea. The Minho district enjoys a normal maritime climate. In the neighbouring province of Trás-os-Montes the winters are severe and the summers excessively hot, with a milder climate in some of the valleys. In coastal Beira the climate is mild, but grows increasingly severe as one moves farther east away from the sea and mounts higher. Extremes of temperature diminish in Estremadura, the province which contains Lisbon, and the country round the capital is famous for its temperate climate. In the Alentejo, on the other hand, south of the Tagus, extremes are violent. The Algarve belongs to that favoured zone of south-west Europe which extends as far as Murcia.

No large river follows a course entirely within Portuguese territory. The Minho, whose bank on the Spanish side is exceedingly rugged, is navigable only beyond Valença do Minho, and is consequently of very little economic importance. Farther south, the picturesque Lima flows into the sea at Viana do Castelo. The Douro (201 miles in Portugal) first follows the frontier, and then flows through a steep valley lined by terraces of vine: on its lower reaches, a few miles from the sea, is the town of Oporto. Not only is it navigable for 125 miles by the *barcos rabelos*, the barges used for transporting the wine, but it supplies the power for important hydro-electric works. The Tagus, which runs for 170 miles through Portugal, is navigable for more than two-thirds of its course, and is also of considerable economic importance. The river, which is between 450 and 550 yards wide and comparatively shallow, broadens out before reaching Lisbon to form the *Mar da Palha*, finally reaching the sea by a channel 9 miles long and $1\frac{1}{4}$ miles wide. The river Sado flows into the bay of Setubal. In the Algarve, the small coastal rivers are of no importance, but the Guadiana, which for 125 miles runs entirely in Portuguese territory, becomes navigable below the gorges of Mertola, at which point it becomes shallow and calm, meandering round numerous islets; its mouth is dotted with fishing smacks and barges laden with copper ore.

Thanks to her geographical situation, Portugal enjoys a great variety of scenery, including frequent tracts of meadow-land rich in various species. The several distinctive regions correspond roughly to the boundaries of the ancient provinces, nowadays replaced by districts. From north to south we have the Minho to the west and Trás-os-Montes to the east, both bordering on Spain; coastal Douro; Beira Alta and Beira Baixa; Estremadura, containing Lisbon; and to the east, along the Tagus, the Ribatejo; next comes the Alentejo, consisting of vast plains stretching between the Tagus and the Algarve; and finally the Algarve in the extreme south.

In the history of Portugal certain governing factors are found to have played a prominent part for as long as the nation has existed as a separate entity. The country had first to be won back from the Moors; but the Moors after their expulsion have left a lasting imprint on dress, habitat, language and race. Once again they had to be fought in Africa. War against the infidel has been one of the permanent factors in Portuguese history. Another age-long epic has been the struggle with Castile: *a priori* nothing required Galicia to form part of Spain, and Portugal to be independent. But the eyes of the future kingdom, unlike their neighbours', were turned seaward, and its people nourished an unconquerable love of liberty: thus it was that what were perhaps, to begin with, merely distinguishing features became the *raison d'être* of independence. Cut off from the east, which in any case offered few attractions, Portugal pursued her greatness on the sea. The Atlantic thus became the third constant factor in the national history.

In Portugal there are but few surviving remains of the cave era. To compensate, during the first millennium B.C. the Lusitanians, who were of partly Celtic origin, built the fortified hill-cities known as *citânias*. The Phoenicians, sailing along the coast, founded commercial settlements. They in turn were supplanted by the Carthaginians, whose presence in the peninsula led to the Roman conquest. The Lusitanians put up a vigorous resistance: Viriathus (the Portuguese Vercingetorix) fought with success against the Romans, only to die by the assassin's hand in 139 B.C. After the settlement of Augustus the peninsula enjoyed the *Pax Romana*. Under the name of Lusitania the future Portugal adopted the language, religion and laws of the conqueror. A certain number of buildings remain to preserve the memory of Roman times.

The barbarian invasions of the fifth century ended in the foundation of the Visigoth kingdom, which collapsed when the Muslims landed in Spain in 711. By the beginning of the eighth century the entire country south of the Vouga was occupied. But the invaders met with a swift resistance. At Covadonga, as early as 718, the men of the Oviedo mountains had won a first victory. This triumph set in motion the reconquest, in the course of which Spain achieved unity and discovered her destiny, while Portugal seized the opportunity to assert her independence.

The small border lands captured from the Muslims in the second half of the eighth century, but still a dependency of the kingdom of Galicia and Leon, were continuously expanded. In 1140 the Moors were driven south of the Mondego, in 1190 the valley of the Tagus was recaptured, and in 1249 the whole of the Algarve was occupied. Thus by the end of the thirteenth century Portugal took shape within what are practically her present-day frontiers. With the growth of the liberated territories the great feudal families increased their power, and gradually contrived to free themselves from dependence on the central authority. In 1095 Alfonso VI of Leon appointed his son-in-law Henry of Burgundy, who was of French origin, governor of the duchy lying between the rivers Minho and Douro. Henry's son Afonso Henriques refused to acknowledge the guardianship of his mother, and in 1143 forced Alfonso VII to recognize his country's independence: he thus became the first King of Portugal (1128–1185). His immediate successors, Sancho I (1185–1211) and Afonso II (1211–1223), with the help of the Military Orders strengthened their control over the coast. Sancho II (1223–1248) and Afonso III (1248–1279) extended their sway up to the Algarve, which was conquered in 1249. The internal organization of the new State was carried out by Diniz (1279–1325). Afonso IV (1325–1357), Pedro I—better known as Pedro the Cruel (1357–1367)—and Ferdinand I. Nevertheless, the struggle against the claims of Castile went on, and may be illustrated by two partly legendary but significant incidents. Afonso Henriques, while besieged in Guimarães, had promised allegiance to Alfonso VII of Leon, and the Portuguese nobleman Egaz Moniz had pledged his sovereign's word. Afonso, however, broke his promise. Egaz Moniz went with his family to Toledo and placed himself in the hands of Alfonso VII, who pardoned him. Even better known is the tragic story of the love affair of Pedro the Cruel. While still heir to the throne he fell madly in love with Inez de Castro, lady-in-waiting to his wife, the

Infanta Constance of Castile. But Inez was herself a Castilian and a member of a powerful family. Fearful of the intrigues of Afonso's brothers, his counsellors—Alvaro Gonçalves, Pero Coelho and Diogo Lopes Pacheco—persuaded the king to sacrifice Inez, and she was assassinated. Pedro, on ascending the throne, got possession of Alvaro Gonçalves and Pero Coelho, tortured them and put them to death. He claimed that Inez had been his lawful wife, and the story tells how he had her body exhumed and conveyed from Coimbra to Alcobaça, where he invested it with the regalia, and forced the courtiers to pay it homage and the nobles to kiss the hand of the 'dead queen' seated at his side.

Ferdinand I committed the serious mistake of giving his daughter and heir Beatrix in marriage to John I, King of Castile. On Ferdinand's death, the extremely unpopular Queen Mother Eleanor became Regent. As the result of a conspiracy, John, Grand Master of the Order of Aviz and a bastard son of Pedro the Cruel, seized the throne. The King of Castile laid siege to Oporto, but was compelled to retire. The Coimbra Cortes proclaimed John of Aviz King of Portugal.[1] A second Castilian invasion was shattered at Albujarrota in 1385 by the Constable Nuño Alvares Pereira.

John I (1385–1433) founded the dynasty of Aviz which lasted for two glorious and prosperous centuries, Portugal's golden age. Like his successors he had the intelligence to see that the future of his country lay not on the Continent, where Castile was a too near and powerful neighbour, but on the sea, which promised infinite possibilities. Trade between Europe and the East was disturbed by the Turks and the Barbary pirates, and it was imperative to find some alternative route to the Mediterranean.

Maritime expansion continued side by side with the struggle between the kings and their too powerful nobles. The Infante Henry the Navigator captured Ceuta. At Sagres, Lagos and Cape St Vincent he encouraged expeditions and revolutionized the science of navigation. Even before his death Madeira, the Azores, Cape Verde and the Gulf of Guinea were occupied or explored. King Duarte (1433–1438) encouraged his brother

[1] John I, by marrying Philippa of Lancaster, secured the alliance with England which has become traditional in Portuguese policy. Their sons are the 'Great Infantes' of Camoëns's poem.

Henry's undertakings, and after his death the Infante Pedro, Regent during the minority of Afonso V (1438–1481), attacked the privileges of the nobility, but was defeated and slain at Alfarrobeira in 1449. Afonso's reign saw the occupation of Alcacer, Arzila and Tangier, and the arrival of a joint Portuguese-Norwegian expedition in Greenland. John II, known as the Perfect Prince, Portugal's greatest king, energetically suppressed the attempts at independence of the great nobles: the Duke of Braganza, the descendant of a bastard son of John I, was executed in 1484. Meanwhile, in the Gulf of Guinea, Diogo de Azambuja built the castle of Mina, Bartolomeu Dias rounded the Cape of Good Hope, and part of the east coast of Africa was explored. The year 1492 saw the discovery of Labrador. The king, while encouraging the science of navigation, rejected Christopher Columbus's plan of reaching the Indies by the eastern route. At Tordesillas in 1494 the Borgia Pope Alexander VI divided all future discoveries between the two Iberian kingdoms, and Portugal was allotted all lands east of a line joining the poles and running 370 miles west of the Cape Verde Isles. Thus Portugal retained Brazil, which had already been discovered and was officially taken over in 1500 by Alvares Cabral.

King Manuel I (1495–1521) achieved the conquest of the West Indies. In 1497–1499 Vasco da Gama rounded South Africa and brought back a cargo of spices. In 1509 Francisco de Almeida destroyed the Venetian and Egyptian fleets; in 1512 Afonso de Albuquerque captured Goa, Malabar, Malacca and the Moluccas; and in 1514 an expedition reached China. In 1520 Ferdinand de Magalão set out on the first voyage round the world, and in the reign of John III (1521–1557) the Portuguese reached Japan.

In literature, these maritime discoveries inspired *The Lusiads* of Camoëns. Owing to the transformation of nautical science and the discovery of the ocean routes by the Portuguese the destinies of western Europe were changed.

But the size of the Portuguese empire was out of proportion to that of the mother country, and the prosperity resulting from such an access of wealth proved partly illusory: moreover, the expulsion of the Jews dealt a blow to the economic system of the country. The struggle against the infidel in Africa became involved in Portugal's policy of empire, and the young king, Sebastian (1557–1578), was lost in the disastrous expedition of Alcacer-Kebir. This was, indeed, more than a military defeat: the fate of the dynasty, and with it the cause of independence, was irreparably compromised. Cardinal Henry, great-uncle of the missing prince, was proclaimed Regent and then King (1578–1580). As he was unwilling or unable to decide between the various claimants to the throne, Philip II of Spain prevailed and received the crown of Portugal from the Cortes at Tomar in 1581.

This event might well have resulted in the union of Portugal with Spain. However, Philip II, by forbidding Dutch vessels to enter the port of Lisbon, brought about the ruin of Portuguese prosperity. The Dutch took possession of the Portuguese empire. Furthermore, the government of Castile, accustomed to forcing unity on the ancient kingdoms of Spain, crushed the country with taxes and reduced it to the status of a province. Away to the east of the peninsula Catalonia seized the opportunity afforded by the struggle between France and Philip IV to rise in revolt. On 1st December 1640 the Portuguese nobles in their turn disowned the house of Hapsburg and proclaimed the accession of the Duke of Braganza, who took the name of John IV (1640–1656). The Spaniards were defeated at Montijo in 1644, but despite French aid, given first openly and then in secret after the Peace of the Pyrenees, it was not until 1668 that the Madrid government recognized the independence of the kingdom of Portugal. Meanwhile, the Portuguese in Brazil had risen against the Dutch, recaptured Angola and São Thomé, and once more united to the mother country, had at least partially restored the lost empire.

Afonso VI, who reigned from 1656 to 1668 but was deposed for cruelty and incapacity, and Pedro II, Regent until 1683 during his brother's lifetime and then king from 1683 to 1706, relied on England to restore their country's place among the great powers. The price exacted was heavy: Bombay was ceded in 1661 as the Infanta Catherine's dowry on her marriage to Charles II, and the country's economic independence was signed away by the Methuen Treaty of 1703.

Introduction

The reign of John V (1706–1750) was remarkable for the unparalleled splendour provided by the riches of Brazil, and demanded by the extravagant tastes of the king. Under Joseph I (1750–1777) and his powerful Minister the Marquès de Pombal, Portugal was ruled by an enlightened despotism which, though frequently odious, brought great benefits to the State. The nobles were held in check, the Duke of Aveiro and his family were tortured and executed, and the Jesuits expelled. The earthquake of 1755, which destroyed Lisbon, provided Pombal with the opportunity of exercising his genius in rebuilding the city. The dictatorship failed to survive the death of the King. Queen Maria I (1777–1792) fell ill, and her son, the future John VI, acted as Regent. Portugal, involved in the European wars, dreaded the spread of revolutionary ideas, and was economically tied to England. In 1793 she was allied to Spain against France. In 1801, Spain having changed sides, she lost Olivença, which she was never afterwards to recover. Napoleon and Godoy in cynical partnership then worked out schemes of partition at Portugal's expense. The country was invaded. The Regent and the royal family, fleeing before Junot's army, sailed in 1807 for Brazil, where they remained until 1821, and Junot entered the capital. In 1808 Soult captured Oporto. Two years later, however, Wellington defeated Masséna at Torres Vedras and forced him to retreat to Spain.

The absence of the royal family fostered the growth of liberal and democratic ideas in the mother country; its residence in Brazil, on the other hand, enabled that country to acquire the apparatus of independent government. John VI, on his return in 1820, was compelled by an insurrection to swear to observe a liberal constitution: but in 1822 Brazil proclaimed its independence and adopted the King's eldest son as the Emperor Pedro I. It was inevitable that the secession of Brazil should bring about serious economic disturbance in Portugal, where the spread of the new ideas had already given rise to political unrest. All the troubles of Portugal in the nineteenth century derive from this source. In Spain the absolutists put forward Don Carlos and the liberals Isabella II, and in Portugal the rival factions followed suit by each adopting a different ruler. On the death of John VI, Pedro retained the crown of Brazil while abandoning that of Portugal to his daughter Maria II under the regency of his brother Miguel. Miguel, however, with the support of the absolutists, usurped the throne from his niece. England supported the liberal party, Pedro restored his daughter, Miguel was driven into exile, and Maria II finally triumphed and reigned from 1834 to 1853. During the reigns of Pedro V (1855–1861), Luis I (1861–1889) and Carlos I (1889–1908) frequent political unrest did not prevent the creation of a new empire in Mozambique and Angola. The continuance of party strife and anarchy led King Carlos to call John Franco to power. The strong measures employed by the latter brought about a violent reaction: the King and the Crown Prince were assassinated in Lisbon in the Praça do Comercio before the eyes of Queen Amelia. After reigning for two years the young King Manuel II was forced to abdicate, and in 1910 the Republic was proclaimed. The new régime, which sent its army to fight in France during the First World War, proved incapable of bringing either order or prosperity to the country. In 1926 a military rising took place, and in 1932 General (afterwards Marshal) Carmona called on Dr Salazar, a professor of Coimbra University. Since then the government has made enormous efforts to modernize the country's economy, and has successfully undertaken the many admirable public works such as roads, bridges and housing.

The most noteworthy buildings surviving from the period of Roman rule are to be found at Evora, where the slim white columns of the Temple of Diana still stand out against the sky.[1] An interesting monument of the pre-Romanesque period is the church of São Frutuoso near Braga. Romanesque art, which flourished at a time when many Portuguese bishops were of French origin, reveals the powerful influence of Cluny, the Auvergne or Languedoc. The principal surviving examples of this style are the cathedrals of Braga (1096–1109), Oporto and Lamego—all of which have undergone a certain amount of alteration—of Coimbra— the best preserved—of Lisbon and of Evora (1186–1283). Their severe style suited the national temperament. Hence, while Gothic flourished

---

[1] For a more detailed account of Portuguese art see *L'Art portugais* by Reynaldo dos Santos (Paris, 1953), a work to which we are greatly indebted.

Introduction

elsewhere, Romanesque continued into the thirteenth century and bequeathed to Portuguese Gothic a notable tendency towards sturdiness and austerity. Alcobaça is a building purely Cistercian in style, though remarkable for the spirited architecture of its church. Batalha reflects the various stages in the evolution of Gothic, and sometimes approaches the English Perpendicular style. The Carmo Convent in Lisbon was, before the devastation caused by the earthquake of 1755, a religious edifice of vast extent. The cathedral of Silves in the Algarve was built after the reconquest of the province in 1279.

The round church of the Templars in Tomar (twelfth century) occupies a place apart as a specimen of the peculiar architecture of the Order and is of the greatest interest owing to its excellent state of preservation and the rarity of churches of this type.

None of the above-mentioned buildings, though in various degrees characteristic of the national style, is unique in the evolution of art. Very different is the case of the monuments of the Manueline period. M. Reynaldo dos Santos, in a generally accepted and extremely attractive theory, postulates a close connection with the great discoveries, to which he attributes their marine symbolism and ornament, crossed with a powerful lyrical strain: he would describe them as the architectural equivalent of *The Lusiads*. This theory has now been vigorously attacked, notably by M. P.-A. Evin[1] who, while acknowledging the inestimable value of the new attributions resulting from M. dos Santos's researches, categorically denies, after an objective analysis of these buildings, any nautical influence. No doubt Portuguese art exhibits the undeniable psychological antipathy of an isolated people towards continental refinements; but further than this we cannot go. The ornamentation has nothing to do with the sea. The so-called ship-cables are in reality nothing more than the rope-mouldings often employed in Late Gothic; while the numerous motifs identified by some writers with fishing tackle are more probably artistic extravagances or hymns of praise to the cork-oak, the sap and the earth.

---

[1] We are grateful to M. P.-A. Evin, who has kindly placed at our disposal his as yet unpublished book on Manueline art.

Moreover, Manueline art derives more from sculpture than from architecture. Its masterpieces consist in what M. Evin calls a kind of 'bloc décoratif appliqué'. Its profound inspiration, while constituting a continuation of Gothic, does not repudiate its Romanesque heritage. It might be described as a Portuguese variant of Flamboyant, an outburst of Baroque—but beneath the unexpected ornamentation the structure remains faithful to tradition.

Comparisons have been drawn between Manueline and the Spanish Plateresque. Both belong rather to the decorative than the architectural realm; both, at the same epoch, are the swan-song of Gothic. But their spirit differs profoundly. Manueline loves sculptural relief and movement, while Plateresque is content to take over motifs from the goldsmith's art and treat them in a quieter style, and with a minimum of relief.

The reign of King Manuel embraces two somewhat different periods of the art which bears his name. This art took shape at Beja, where the future monarch and his sister Leonor were brought up: the remains of the ducal palace and of the convent of Conceição are a reminder of this origin. The first period is that of the architect Boytac, perhaps a Frenchman from Languedoc, and reveals an agreeable and sufficiently sober style. Boytac built the church of Jesus at Setubal, worked on the monastery of Santa Cruz in Coimbra, built the nave and cloisters of the church at Belem, and was also responsible for the cloister-screens and the Unfinished Chapels at Batalha. This first period had an interesting sequel at Coimbra thanks to Marcos Pires, who himself also worked on the Santa Cruz Monastery and built the University Chapel. The palace of Sintra marks the transition to the second, livelier and more dramatic period, during which Francisco de Arruda built the Tower of Belem, while his brother Diogo was responsible for the Manueline works of art at Tomar, in particular the celebrated Chapter House window. But King Manuel seems to have broken away from this, and deliberately to have let in a breath of the Renaissance. The Arruda brothers, however, continued working for him, though only on works of military art. We note, lastly, that Mateus Fernandes designed the porch of the Unfinished Chapels at Batalha. The whole of these astonishing buildings are frequently surmounted or decorated by the Cross of the Order of Christ and the armillary sphere of King Manuel.

The Renaissance, in the reign of John III, boasted of artists such as the Castilhos from Biscay, or Nicolas Chanterène and Jean de Rouen from France, the last two being principally sculptors. In this period the new art flourished in various centres—Coimbra, Evora and Tomar. In Tomar, João de Castilho added to the already wonderful convent of the Order of Christ, while a little lower down the hill on which the monastery stands Diogo de Torralva built the small church of the Conception, remarkable for the perfection of its lines.

In the last quarter of the sixteenth century the Italian Filippo Terzi, who worked in Portugal from 1576 to 1587, built the aqueducts at Vila do Conde, Coimbra and Tomar, as well as the church of São Vicente in Lisbon and probably the Episcopal Palace at Coimbra.

In the seventeenth century, during the Baroque period, families of architects such as the Turrianos and Tinoccos carried out restorations and additions to many churches and monasteries. The first half of the following century saw great changes, due to the lavish and Italianate tastes of John V. The German Frederic Ludwig built the monastery palace of Mafra, Baroque in style but rivalling the Escorial in size. The same artistic tendencies developed at Evora, where the architect transformed the cathedral choir. Ludwig's pupils, Reinaldo Manuel and Mateus Vicente, built the palace of Queluz near Lisbon, and the Estrêla Church in the capital itself.

The earthquake of 1755 led to the birth, in the second half of the century, of a new 'Pombaline' Lisbon, built on a geometrical plan. The Praça do Comercio, with its statue of King Joseph by Machado de Castro, is planned along the lines of a French 'place royale'.

In the north, however, and particularly in Oporto, we come upon a local Baroque whose master was Nicholas Nazzoni (1732–1773). In Oporto he built the Torre dos Clerigos (1738–1748) and the side loggia of the cathedral (1736).

One of the most original features of Portuguese art to attract the tourist is the number of carved and gilded retables to be found in the churches.

Though similar in appearance to Spanish retables, they nevertheless have a distinctive character of their own, belonging to sculpture in their profusion of ornament, and to architecture in the grandeur of their design. Such was their popularity in the seventeenth and eighteenth centuries that specimens are to be found in almost every Romanesque and Gothic church. In the sixteenth century and the first half of the seventeenth, the Renaissance style predominates; towards the middle of the seventeenth century a change takes place, and by 1675–1700 the riot of Baroque ornament gains ground. The Churrigueras retables of Spain are so overloaded with ornament as to smother the leading lines of the design, and architecture dissolves into decoration; moreover, their main function is to frame a picture or a statue. The Portuguese retable, on the other hand, is no mere framework but a doorway or triumphal arch requiring no centre-piece in the shape of picture or statue: their architectural design never becomes lost or confused. They are in fact a translation into carved and gilded wood, suitable to a church interior, of the doorways of the Romanesque period.

In the eighteenth century, under the influence of the Italianate taste of John V and thanks to the wealth of Brazil, this *talha durada* or gilt woodcarving overflows the walls and ceiling of the churches. In short, they display the same passion for carved and richly decorated woodwork as we find in the carvings on the royal coaches, of which José de Almeida was the most famous sculptor.

Neither the geometric ornamentation of the Romanesque doorways nor the somewhat rare statuary of the Gothic doorways reach such a perfection of beauty as the medieval tombs of Portugal. To the first third of the fourteenth century belong the tomb of the queen, Saint Isabella, which was transferred from the old to the new convent of Santa Clara in Coimbra, and the wonderful tomb of Gonzalo Pereira, Archbishop of Braga, by Pero de Coimbra and Telo Garcia, the gem of the cathedral of the old religious capital. To about 1360 belong the tombs of Pedro the Cruel and Inez de Castro, now in the monastery of Alcobaça. These, though showing signs of French influence, are purely Portuguese in their

Introduction

decorative motifs and in the story which they commemorate, and are perhaps the masterpiece of Portuguese medieval sculpture. To the fifteenth century belong the royal or princely tombs of Batalha, and to the end of the same century the tombs erected by Diogo Pires the elder at São Marcos near Coimbra.

We have already referred to Manueline sculpture in connection with the contemporary architecture with which it is closely associated. At the time of the Renaissance, Nicolas Chanterène, Jean de Rouen and Hodart deserve a mention owing to their French origin as well as their genius. Chanterène, artist and courtier, a refined and Italianate humanist, began his career in Portugal in January 1517, when he was commissioned to undertake the main doorway of the church of Belem, in which his principal work was the kneeling statues of King Manuel and Queen Maria, whose design is not unlike that of Champmol. From 1518 to about 1530 he worked at Coimbra. In the monastery of Santa Cruz he is responsible for the recumbent effigies of Afonso Henriques and Sancho I (1518–1520) in the choir, for the famous pulpit (1521), and in about the year 1523 for the statues on the main façade of the cathedral designed by Diogo de Castilho. In the same period he sculptured the great retable of the high altar of São Marcos, on the outskirts of the city, and in 1526 the choir door of the monastery at Celas. His hand may also be discerned in the *porta especiosa*, built about 1530, a charming structure with several tiers of loggias. In 1531 and 1532 we find him at Sintra, commissioned by John III to sculpt the great alabaster retable for the high altar of the Pena Palace chapel. From 1533 to 1540 Evora was the centre of his activities: the pillars of the convent of Paraiso (1533), the tomb of Alvarez de Costa (1535) in the same convent, the tombs of Francisco de Melo in the church of the Loios, and of Afonso of Portugal in the Graça Church (1537)—all works of consummate beauty, now moved to the town museum, except the last-named, which has been allowed to remain in the church. Finally, at some time before 1548 he sculpted the tomb of Jorge de Melo, bishop of Portalegre, now in the monastery of Conceiçao.

A very different artist is Jean de Rouen, who was primarily a carver, with a far greater appeal to popular taste. He arrived in Coimbra shortly before 1530 and after the departure of Chanterène, and with the help of his pupils, filled the churches and monasteries of the Mondego valley with a charming efflorescence of works hewn from the local Ança stone. The retable at Varziela, dating from about 1530, is perhaps his masterpiece: the retable of Guarda Cathedral (about 1550–1553) already shows signs of commercialization, and is decidedly inferior. Between these two extremes he produced a number of pleasing and poetical works in a style very different from that of Chantarène.

The tragic and tempestuous genius of Hodart derives neither from humanism nor from popular taste. He worked at Toledo from 1522 to 1526, and seems to have collaborated in the Puerta del Perdón of Seville Cathedral. From 1530 on we find him in Coimbra, where the impressive fragments of his enormous *Last Supper* are preserved in the Machado de Castro Museum. Hodart was more than a gifted artist, he was a tremendous personality.

In the eighteenth century, during the Baroque period, two very different tendencies are noticeable; first, the polychrome terra-cotta sculpture of the monks of Alcobaça, highly charged with emotion, which follows the national tradition, and secondly, the huge statues at Mafra, imported from Italy, which set a pattern for the next generation whose greatest artist was Machado de Castro. We have already mentioned José de Almeida in connection with the gilded wooden retables.

Soares dos Reis, Teixera Lopes in the nineteenth century, and Francisco Franco in our own day, have upheld the national traditions of sculpture.

Portuguese painting begins with the Primitives of the period 1450–1550 during the greatest days of the Aviz dynasty. The late arrival of the Renaissance explains their survival well into the sixteenth century.

In the third quarter of the fifteenth century Nuno Gonçalves painted the polyptych of *The Veneration of St Vincent*, in which courtiers, monks of Alcobaça, fishermen and dukes of Braganza are grouped around the patron saint of Lisbon. This huge and splendid work, which once adorned the altar of St Vincent in Lisbon Cathedral, is now in the Museum of Ancient Art. Of striking originality even when compared with Flemish painting (Jan van Eyck visited Portugal in 1428 with the embassy sent by Philip the Good to seek the hand of the Infanta Isabella), it has never been surpassed in its own country, and remains one of the most marvellous creations of European art. Around Nuno Gonçalves are grouped a number of other painters with whose work we shall become acquainted in Lisbon and elsewhere.

In succession to this inspired artist we may note, in the first half of the sixteenth century in the reigns of Manuel and John III, two painters of Flemish origin; Francisco Henriques, who is known to have flourished between 1500 and 1518, and Frei Carlos, a monk of Evora who worked from 1517 to 1540. During this period Flanders sent to Portugal not only works of art (King Manuel placed many orders in Flanders, and imported a great retable by Quentin Metsys for the Madre de Deus Convent in Lisbon), but also artists who were quick to adapt themselves to the local genius. Mention must be made of two art centres, Lisbon and Viseu. In Lisbon the most prominent painter was Jorge Afonso; his pupils included his son-in-law Gregorio Lopes, Cristovão de Figueiredo, Garcia Fernandes who in 1518 married a daughter of Francisco Henriques, and lastly Pero and Gaspar Vaz. In Viseu, Vasco Fernandes (known as the Grão Vasco) displayed the lofty and moving talent which raised him high above the level of his contemporaries. Gaspar Vaz also worked in the Viseu district. This select band of artists, despite a more or less pronounced Flemish influence, show undeniable originality—a sense of drama, a passion for skilful draperies and elaborate landscapes, and a palette mixed with the sea-mist of the Atlantic.

The second half of the sixteenth century is marked by the flowering of the Renaissance and the growing influence of Italy. Cristovão, the son of Gregorio Lopes, is already an Italianizer. To this period also belong Gaspar and Fernão Gomes.

The seventeenth century, whose first half passed under the domination of Spain, seems an age of artistic decline. But it must be remembered that several Portuguese artists worked at the Spanish court—and Velazquez himself, after all, was partly of Portuguese descent.

The eighteenth century shows a powerful French influence: both

Quillard and Pillement, for example, visited and worked in Portugal. Domingos Sequeira, who worked well into the nineteenth century, is capable of comparison, by his life and genius, with the great Goya: both led the same troubled life, both suffered for their political beliefs, and both were gifted with a similar inspiration.

Nineteenth-century Portuguese painting, little known abroad, produced one great artist in Columbano, an important collection of whose works is housed in the Lisbon Museum of Modern Art.

This short sketch of Portuguese art would not be complete without a mention of the gold and silver work which constitutes one of the chief treasures displayed in the museums, and of the *azulejos*, or glazed decorative tiles, which have always retained their popularity, especially in the seventeenth and eighteenth centuries.

The Portuguese people, united though they are, reflect the successive deposits upon which the nation has been built up—Lusitanians, Iberians, Celts, Greeks, Romans, Suevians, Visigoths and Moors. The population of eight millions offers some striking contrasts: the densely inhabited districts of Oporto, Braga and Aveiro, the apparently empty spaces of the Alentejo, bare-footed peasants in their black clothes, American cars, tiny white houses wreathed in flowers, vast flats in the modern quarter of Lisbon. ... So much for the country's land and history: the time has come to set out on the successive stages of our journey.

1. FEMME DE PÊCHEUR
FISHERMAN'S WIFE

2. LE TAGE.
   THE TAGUS.

3. LISBONNE. JARDINS DU PALACIO FRONTEIRA.
   LISBON. GARDENS OF THE PALACIO FRONTEIRA.

4. PRÈS DE NAZARÉ.
   NEAR NAZARÉ.

5. NORIA.

6. SUR LE MONDEGO.
   ON THE MONDEGO.

7. SCÈNES TYPIQUES DE LA VIE...
TYPICAL SCENES OF THE LIFE...

8. ...DANS LES VILLAGES DE LA CÔTE OUEST.
...IN THE VILLAGES OF THE WEST COAST.

9. ÉGLISE DE LOURINHÃ.
    SAINT JEAN À PATMOS.
    CHURCH OF LOURINHÃ.
    SAINT JOHN AT PATMOS.

10. MUSÉE DE VISEU.
    VASCO FERNANDES. DÉTAIL DU CALVAIRE.
    MUSEUM OF VISEU.
    VASCO FERNANDES. DETAIL FROM THE CALVARY.

CHAPTER I

Oporto and the Northern Districts

THREE provinces radiate from Oporto: coastal Douro, Trás-os-Montes and Minho, with their respective capitals Oporto, Vila Real and Braga. They differ not only in appearance but in their economy and traditional customs.

Situated in the extreme north-east and jutting into Spanish territory, Trás-os-Montes, seldom visited and presenting many archaic features, is one of the most attractive districts in Portugal. Dry and sparsely inhabited, it consists of a collection of river-basins, fractures and narrow valleys. The climate is severe, with long snow-bound winters and burning summers. The peasants make a living less from agriculture properly so-called than from stock-rearing or from tending their flocks.

Many an outlandish village is to be found in Trás-os-Montes. Protected apparently for centuries from any outside influence, they have retained intact their immemorial customs: in one, bride-abduction is practised; in another, on Good Friday, Death descends on the village, cracking his whip and brandishing a trident. Clothes are of homespun, often of a freakish pattern. Everything in this province, whether the prevailing colour of the countryside be brown or reddish, expresses a majestic austerity, though prosperous farms are to be found in the vicinity of Mirandela, Chaves or Vila Real.

Miranda do Douro, facing the Spanish frontier, is one of the province's most picturesque towns. Across the river lies the age-long enemy, Spain. The cathedral, built by Miguel de Arruda, commands a wonderful prospect. It would be greatly to our delight if, in addition to admiring the beauties of art and nature, we could somehow become acquainted with the private life of the inhabitants. We watch them go by in their frieze jackets, their faces tanned by the wind and looking even swarthier

II. COIMBRA
    RETABLE DU MAÎTRE-AUTEL DE LA CATHÉDRALE
    RETABLE OF THE HIGH ALTAR OF THE CATHEDRAL

under the brims of their caps. The muslin collars of the women cast a floral pattern on the black stones, the stick-dances remind us of Spanish castanets. In the Miranda district the people still retain their traditional dress and local dialect.

Braganza was once the capital of the dukes of that name who provided Portugal with her last dynasty. Its towers and double surrounding walls stand out among the wind-swept peaks of a stern landscape. Inside the walls there are many interesting buildings: the Tower of Homage and the remains of the castle of Sancho I, the Gothic pillory, the sixteenth-century church of Santa Maria, and above all the granite Romanesque Town Hall with its noble flight of semicircular arches.

Mirandela, with its girdle of ramparts and towers, forms a striking contrast to Vila Real, with its wealth of emblazoned houses and its noisy, animated market. A visit to Vila Real must include the church of São Domingos, whose Gothic style retains a delightful and characteristic flavour of Romanesque. From the promenade facing the cemetery there is a wild and impressive view over the gorges of the Cabril and the Corgo. But the most charming memory remains that of the castle of the counts of Vila Real, a few kilometres outside the town: the harmony of the delicate colours under the blue of the sky, the graceful treatment of the window arches and the proportions of the façades are a revelation of the exquisite loveliness of Portuguese Baroque.

In the south of the province, near the bare and wretched uplands of Montemuro where the children spring up from the road to beg for alms, lies the little town of Lamego, comely and smiling and typical of so many other towns which we shall have occasion to admire in the course of our travels. It is dominated by two distant pine-girt heights, on one of which stands the castle and the old quarter, on the other the church of Nossa Senhora dos Remedios. This sanctuary, dating from the mid-eighteenth century and the scene of a highly popular pilgrimage, is spread over the surrounding woods, and includes monumental staircases, statues and a Baroque church. The general effect, like that of the Bom Jesus in Braga, reminds us of some nobleman's seat set in a smiling park and graciously given over by the owner to the Sunday devotions of the peasantry. As one mounts or descends the imposing steps one is always expecting to encounter a master who is not The Lord. . . .

In the lower town the cathedral, which has suffered extensive alteration, and the old bishop's palace containing the museum are separated by flower-beds, and form a centre such as is usually to be found in any small Portuguese town. The museum contains a few sixteenth-century Brussels tapestries, almost unique in Portugal, but unfortunately completely faded: their main subjects are the story of Oedipus, and *Music*, part of the popular series representing the Deadly Sins. There is also an even more damaged set of Lebrun's *Alexander*, a coarse specimen of Aubusson work which could never have ranked as a masterpiece. Nevertheless the museum is worth a visit for the freshness of its local sculpture, and the charm, at once rustic and refined, of its restored Baroque chapels of carved and gilded wood. In the old days the bishops were powerful men and patrons of the arts: their sedan-chairs and coaches are on view in the museum. The gem of the collection is the remains of the cathedral's ancient retable, the work of Grão Vasco (1506–1511). The *Annunciation*, the *Visitation*, the *Circumcision*, the *Creation of the Animals* are, or at any rate the first three, among the finest pictures of Vasco, who worked chiefly at near-by Viseu in the province of Beira. Some Flemish influence seems to have inspired the room where Mary and the angel converse to all eternity, and the temple in which the rite of circumcision is performed. Yet it is Vasco's sensibility that breathes life into the sacred characters, and instils pathos into the charming landscape of the *Visitation*: and the same emotions can be felt in the first cry, the first stirring of the animals as they issue from the hand of their Creator.[1]

No visitor to Trás-os-Montes should rest content with a hurried itinerary, or limit himself to a few towns and local customs. There are many surprises to repay the attentive traveller. There are spas at Vidago and Pedras Salgadas, and towns little known to the tourist but attractive for all that, such as Chaves with its Roman bridge, and Murça with its

---

[1] A few miles from Lamego, but in the adjacent province of Beira Alta, there is a retable in the church of Feirreirim executed in collaboration by Cristovão de Figueiredo, Garcia Fernandes, Gregorio Lopez and Cristovão of Utrecht. It dates from 1533 to 1536.

amazing iron-age Pig Statue: the natives of this savage and splendid district delight in tales of horror; the story goes that the countryside was ravaged by a monstrous boar which was destroyed by the local lord, whereupon the grateful peasants set up this enigmatic monument....

There is a striking contrast between the two provinces of Trás-os-Montes and Minho. As we approach the sea there is a change from rugged mountains and homespun clothes and legends of violence to green and fresh uplands, exuberant festivals and bright costumes.

The province of Minho, well stocked with rivers and close to the Atlantic, is remarkable, in spite of its soft blue sky, for its local haze. Vegetation is abundant. Maize grows sometimes to the banks of the Minho; half-way up, the mountains are covered in green, the road is shaded by trees, and flowers bloom everywhere still moist from the latest dews or rain. The granite houses, with stairways clinging to the walls and balconies supported by stone pillars, are partly covered in vines; for this is the *vinho verde* country, where the vine-stocks climb up plants and walls, giving the landscape a very different appearance from the vineyards of the Douro. On our way we meet teams of oxen under their skilfully painted yokes, pulling wicker carts, a bucolic scene breathing the very spirit of the peaceful countryside.

Minho indeed is the province of poetry, of country dances, of splendid folklore, of the *romaria*—part processional pilgrimage, part fair, and part travelling *festa*—and of flowered aprons flaunting on the women's hips.

To get from Trás-os-Montes we are obliged, owing to the roughness of the mountain roads, to leave the Spanish frontier and proceed by way of Vila Real and Braga.

On our way, Guimarães is a reminder of the glorious history of the birth of the Portuguese nation. Its castle, whose majestic turrets still stand out against the sky, was the birthplace of Afonso Henriques, who was baptized in the adjoining Romanesque chapel. Henry of Burgundy and his son rebuilt the abbey of Nossa Senhora da Oliveira, whose church was subsequently rebuilt by John I and, in the sixteenth century, by the Cogominho family; but the cloister and chapter-house still bear witness to the patronage of Henry and Afonso. The monastery treasure is now housed in the Alberto Sampeiro Museum: the triptych-reliquary of The Nativity was said to have been captured from the King of Castile's tent at the battle of Albujarrota—actually it was commissioned by John I in fulfilment of a vow made during the battle to the Virgin of Guimarães. The Romanesque chalice decorated with heraldic lions was presented in 1187 by Sancho I and Queen Dulce to Santa Marinha da Costa. There is also a silver-gilt reliquary with Gothic lettering bearing the date 1419, and a monstrance decorated with enamel and bells and angel-musicians, bearing the date 1534. The monastery of São Domingos, less well known than Nossa Senhora da Oliveira, possesses a Gothic church and cloister.

Braga, the see of an archbishop, has a long and stirring history. It was already an important place under the Romans, was captured by the Goths and the Moors, and after the reconquest enjoyed a period of prosperity thanks to Bishop Pedro (1067–1096) and to its first archbishop, St Geraldo (1096–1108). Under Diogo de Sousa, an archbishop in the direct line of the great Renaissance prelates, the city attained a splendour rivalling that of Evora or Coimbra. Unfortunately the taste of his seventeenth- and eighteenth-century successors was less reliable.

The atmosphere of the city, like that of every religious capital, is heavy with incense. Life flows on at a slow pace, in the rhythm of a place which, of its former importance, retains only a spiritual role. It exhales the poetry of churches, monasteries, old streets and fountains. Sometimes of an evening a picturesque or devotional excitement stirs the quarters adjacent to the cathedral: on St John's Day, for example, temporary erections light up the streets with innumerable electric lamps; and on Good Friday a procession of penitents passes through the main streets by night, their blazing torches painting monstrous flowers on the sky, while the sound of their praying-wheels echoes strangely amid the devotions of the populace.

The cathedral, built in the Romanesque style on a Cluniac plan, once revealed a decided Burgundian influence. Of the first period of building nothing remains but the coving of the main portal, the south portal, and the bracketed cornice of the transept and side aisles. In the fourteenth century Archbishop Gonzalo Pereira built the Gothic chapel of Nossa

Senhora da Gloria: his own tomb (1334) by the master-sculptors Pero and Telo Garcia is one of the masterpieces of Portuguese art. In the sixteenth century Archbishop Diogo de Sousa completed the porch of the façade and the restoration of the apse, in whose outside wall stands the enchanting statue of Nossa Senhora da Leite, smiling artlessly beneath her canopy. The rather clumsy towers of the façade were erected in the eighteenth century. The cathedral, the work of many different periods and prelates, gains in mystery what it loses in consistency. The original building is difficult to trace, but there is wonderful charm in the Late Gothic arches of the apse, happily silhouetted against the sky. The interior breathes a sober poetry, and the visitor, gradually transformed into a pilgrim, lights upon one masterpiece after another. First there is the tomb of Gonzalo Pereira, with the archbishop stretched out in preternatural calm, among the most beautiful of medieval recumbent effigies. The panels of the sarcophagus are decorated with scenes from the life of Christ. Over the high altar stands the fourteenth-century statue of Santa Maria de Braga, of French or French-influenced workmanship. On the other hand, the gilt copper tomb of the Infante Afonso, eldest son of John I, is the work of a Flemish artist. Lastly, contrasting with the medieval fabric of the building, the *coro alto* is a vast and sumptuous product of the eighteenth century (1733–1737).

The old bishop's palace is now one of the finest libraries in Portugal. The chapel of the Immaculate Conception is remarkable for its design, a tower with crenellated walls.

No visit to Braga is complete without a leisurely stroll through the old quarters of the town, where humble women dressed in black pass on their way through the streets, summoned by the cathedral bells. Nor should one fail to listen to the ceaseless song of the angels sung by the fountains as they tell their beads against the blue and silent air.

In fact, the whole environs of the town bear witness to its former importance as a religious centre. A visit should be paid to the pre-Romanesque church of São Frutuoso embedded in its convent, or to the ancient Benedictine monastery of Tibães, rebuilt in the seventeenth and eighteenth centuries. But the most popular excursion is to the church of

Bom Jesus do Monte on the top of the Monte Espinho, built in the eighteenth century by Cruz Amarante. Bom Jesus is at one and the same time a wonderful park containing exotic trees, a summer resort, a favourite view—and a pilgrimage church. The architectural staircase, the colossal statues, the bars and hotels convey an atmosphere which, if not entirely frivolous, can scarcely be called religious. Nevertheless, the sight of a band of pilgrims mounting the stairs on their knees suffices to introduce into the peaceful holiday scene a reminder of the tragic story of Christianity. . . .

East of Braga the road leads, not far from Lanheses, to the country seat of the counts of Bertiandos, an exquisite house breathing all the poetry of the province of Minho. The same poetical charm awaits us by the banks of the river, for the road to the north soon brings us to the river Minho. Spanish and Portuguese towns, each defended by fortifications, confront each other across the water, silent witnesses of the many occasions throughout the centuries when the two countries have been at war. Nothing of this now remains but the fortifications, rising from a sea of greenery and staring at the river as it flows lazily beneath a kindly sky. In front of us the cathedral and old town of Tuy stand perched like a granite nosegay on their rock, and on the opposite bank lies Valença do Minho buried in flowers.

We must now descend the Portuguese bank to the mouth of the river, and take one look at the summit of Santa Tecla in Galicia before finally turning our back on Spain and proceeding southward along the coast.

Here is Viana do Castelo, the jewel of the province of Minho. Standing on the right bank of the river Lima, the town rejoices in a wonderful view. It contains a collection of buildings of the first importance; the church of São Domingos with its Renaissance façade and the tomb of Fr. Bartolomeu dos Martires, archbishop of Braga; the parish church whose Middle Gothic design retains a touch of Romanesque severity, and whose doorway recalls the porch of the Gloria of St James of Compostella: and finally the buildings surrounding the Square of the Republic. This square reminds us of Venice in its almost aerial grace: the sixteenth-century Misericordia, in fact, is pierced with arcades and loggias like a palace on the Grand Canal. The church was rebuilt in the eighteenth century in a charming Baroque style. In front of the Town Hall the water splashes from an entrancing fountain erected in 1554. The whole group of buildings, all built within a few years of each other, composes one of the most striking townscapes in Portugal.

Viana is not only the city of lace and embroidery, but the home of Nossa Senhora da Agonia, whose pilgrimage in August provides the occasion for the most splendid of all *festas*. A rain of flowers falls on the streets, decorated with shawls and counterpanes and precious carpets, while a flourish of trumpets and roll of drums greets the interminable and unforgettable procession as it pushes through the dense crowd. In front marches a motley concourse of Biblical patriarchs, allegorical personages, martyrs and saints—the whole pageant of Christendom. The women wear numberless ear-rings, brilliant flowered dresses and aprons which seem, like St Isabella's, to have been strewn with a gift of flowers from heaven. After the claims of religion have been satisfied, every couple joins in the rapid rhythm of the dance.

Not everyone can manage a visit to Viana in August, but at any time of the year one has only to climb to the church of Santa Luzia on the green hill which towers above the town to succumb to the beauty of the scene spread out below—an amazing jumble of belfries and palaces and gardens glittering with the steel-blue spangles showered down from the sun overhead.

Still farther to the south we come to Povoa de Varzim and Vila do Conde, the latter dominated by its aqueduct and the convent of Santa Clara containing a large number of medieval tombs. We are now in the province of Douro Litoral: the road leaves the coast, and an unbroken succession of small towns warns us that we are approaching Oporto.

The province of Douro Litoral contains a wealth of architecture. In Penafiel we pause at the Renaissance parish church. Leça do Bailo possesses a fourteenth-century Templars' fortress-church, with tombs of the knights of Malta and Manueline baptismal fonts. Travanca also deserves a visit. It lies at the bottom of a wooded valley: its Benedictine abbey, founded towards the end of the tenth century, contains a fine chapel, probably of the twelfth century, and the sixteenth-century sacristy contains some astonishing vestments painted in a Chinese style.

But of all the towns in the Douro Litoral only Oporto demands a lengthy visit.

Oporto is the second city of Portugal—to which it gave its name—the second port of the country, and a commercial and industrial centre whose world-famous wines are only one among many other specialities. Oporto was in frequent contact with Flanders, and also, after the Methuen Treaty, with England: indeed, the character of the city has been strongly influenced by the English merchants settled within its walls. By a peculiarity rare in Portugal, life seems to centre on frantic activity, on business and getting rich: the superfluities—such as art—are comparatively neglected. In the steep bustling streets, swarming with American cars, the visitor feels lost and disappointed. An effort has to be made before this after all beautiful city can succeed in touching our emotions.

Its past history, which was glorious if only for the courage shown by the citizens during the liberal revolutionary wars of the last century, seems obliterated by the ultra-modern flats of the Praça da Liberdade and the Avenida dos Aliados. The variety of its activities is obscured by the fame of its wines, though these are as a matter of fact produced from the vines of the upper Douro district, and are only brought to Vila Nova da Gaia across the river to mature.

The magnificence of the city and its site can best be appreciated either from the Maria Pia bridge (1876), the first of its kind to be designed and built by Eiffel, or from the King Luis bridge farther downstream. The huge agglomeration of buildings is piled up in an amphitheatre on the north bank of the Douro, with the cathedral and the Torre dos Clerigos standing out from the mass of houses, stairways and granite churches.

The popular quarters, with their narrow precipitous streets, their dirt and picturesque charm, lie near or on the bank of the river clustered round the cathedral, whose Romanesque architecture was defaced in the seventeenth and eighteenth centuries, though its north façade is embellished with a lovely loggia (1736). The main streets in the centre are worthy of a capital, and the vast works in progress near the São Bento station will change the face of that quarter of the city. Numerous gardens provide a refuge from the noise and bustle surrounding the Santo Antonio hospital.

Such in brief would be the impression left by Oporto if one confined oneself to the hectic contemporary scene. Yet the city boasts of several remarkable buildings like the Romanesque church of Cedofeita, and especially of a dazzling collection of seventeenth- and eighteenth-century wooden sculptures in such churches as São Francisco and São Bento de Vitoria and the convent of Santa Clara. The confraternity of the Santa Casa da Misericordia has a painting of the 'Fons Vitae' attributed to Bernard van Orley: from a fountain filled with the Saviour's blood rises the crucified Christ between the Virgin and St John; King Manuel and Queen Eleanor, together with the children of the King's earlier marriages, kneel before this spectacle whose mystic significance appealed to every Christian soul. The museum which bears the name of the great sculptor Soares dos Reis possesses, among others of this artist's work, his famous picture *The Exile*: it also contains portraits of Marguerite de Valois and of Henry II by François Clouet, and an important collection of sixteenth-century Limoges enamels consisting chiefly of a series representing the Passion, by Jean II Pénicaud after Albrecht Dürer, which came from the monastery of Santa Cruz in Coimbra.

In northern Portugal there is a stretch of country even lovelier than the Minho—the valley of the upper Douro, district of the vines from which port wine is made. On either side of the river, from a point 62 miles upstream from Oporto to the Spanish frontier, stretches 'the producing district of the noble wines of Douro', as it is officially designated by a decree of 1932. In southern Trás-os-Montes, near Beira, the heights north and south of the river and its tributaries hold off the rains and form a barrier against the moist Atlantic wind. There has thus come into existence a natural glass-house, stiflingly hot in summer, where the vines can ripen in the schistose soil. Ever since the sixteenth century the immense labours of man have transformed the two sides of the valley into huge amphitheatres with vine-bearing terraces stepping down to the river-bed hidden in the hollow of the valley.

At vintage time, when the valley is like a furnace, the labourers swarm in from all parts of the surrounding country. Under a blazing sun, in an atmosphere unruffled by the slightest breeze, the wicker baskets must be filled and the heavy load, held by a strap running round the forehead, carried to the proprietor's *quinta*. The heaviest work is carried out by the men. As soon as the vats are full, the vintagers plunge barefooted into the piles of grapes, grip each other round the waist, and begin to tread to the rhythm of a slow dance, while the icy-cold juice oozes between their feet. The must is left a short time to rest and cool off, when work is resumed. At night the treaders relax in a *vira*, a lively quick dance to the accompaniment of concertina and guitar. Once the *corta do lagar*, or treading, is over, the next stage is to fortify the liquid by adding brandy. The wine is not kept on the proprietor's estate, but is first removed in ox-drawn basket-carts and then dispatched to the coast either by rail or by *barcos rabelos*. These traditional Douro barges are shaped like an incense-boat, low and flat and rising to a point at the prow, and fitted with square sails and a huge tiller. By this means the casks reach Vila Nova da Gaia where, after a gap of some dozens of miles, the official Douro wine district begins again. Finally the wine is stored in the immense warehouses across the river from Oporto, where it is carefully tended until it reaches full maturity.

What a wonderful sight are the vineyards of the Douro! In the gaping break between the bends of the mountains the terraces slope down to the river-bed which threads its way far below among the rocks. Wherever the patches of rock break through, their grey tones stand out against the green fields. Part only of the valley-sides is planted with vines, and here and there a field is sandwiched in between. The peace of this vast tract of country is born of the silence which reigns everywhere, and from the harmony established between nature and the works of man. All along the road are belvederes commanding unforgettable views.

In the gorges of Cachão da Valeira, in the infinite panoramas of Pinhão the birds sing, a white wing flashes across the shadow of the tall trees, the perfume of the heavy grapes floats up on every side, and everywhere a purple haze rises and dissolves into thin air. In this peaceful valley, scorched at midday and crimsoned by the setting sun, the vine-dresser has shaped for centuries the scene of his labours, from which he himself seems mysteriously absent.

The only sound to break the silence is the rhythmic cry of the peasant in the next field as he drives his yoke of oxen and traces with his call an arabesque of joy on the tranquil air. In the distance a *barco rabelo* floats before the wind patiently following the river's meandering course, its sail fluttering like a flower among the stones of the Douro.

For several miles eastward and upstream the landscapes are equally magnificent. But with the approach to the Spanish frontier the scenery grows more rugged, the vine fades from the rock, and the already cruel heat of the sun becomes pitiless. Near Barca d'Alva we pass through an unending apocalypse of stony valleys abandoned by men and trees, where even the springs disdain to gush.

The grandeur of the upper Douro can only be described as Biblical, an epithet which becomes all the apter when we consider that man has partly created this landscape with his own hands.

If there be indeed a chosen people, it would find on the slopes of this valley its Promised Land. It is one of the pleasantest districts in all Portugal, surpassing all others in its noble blend of the bounty of nature with the handiwork of man.

12. PAYSAGE DU TRAS-OS-MONTES
LANDSCAPE IN TRAS-OS-MONTES
13. BRAGANZA

14. MIRANDELA.

17. MOISSONS SUR LA ROUTE DE CHAVES.
HARVEST ON THE CHAVES ROAD.

15-16. PRÈS DE MIRANDA DO DOURO.
NEAR MIRANDA DO DOURO.

18. GUIMARÃES.

19. BRAGA. LE BOM JESUS DO MONTE.
THE BOM JESUS DO MONTE.

20

21

20-21-22.
BRAGA. LA CATHÉDRALE.
NOSSA SENHORA DA LEITE,
ET EX-VOTO.
THE CATHEDRAL.
NOSSA SENHORA DA LEITE
AND EX-VOTO.

23-24-25. BRAGA.
FÊTES DE LA SAINT-JEAN.
THE FESTIVAL OF ST JOHN.

VIANA DO CASTEL

26.
PORTAIL DE
L'ÉGLISE PAROISSI
PORTAL OF THE
PARISH CHURCH.

27. PROCE

28. ENVIRONS DE PONTE DO LIMA.
AROUND PONTE DO LIMA.

29. POVOA DE VARZIM.
POISSON SÉCHANT AU SOLEIL.
FISH DRYING IN THE SUN.

30. PORTO.
OPORTO.

31. PORTO. LE PONT DOM LUIS I.
OPORTO. THE DOM LUIS I BRIDGE.

32. A PORTO.
AT OPORTO.

33-34.
L'ANCIEN ET LE
NOUVEAU PORTO.
THE OLD AND
NEW OPORTO.

35. ÉGLISE DES CARMES.   PORTO.   36. FONTAINE SÃO SEBASTIÃO.
    CARMELITE CHURCH.   OPORTO.   THE SÃO SEBASTIAO FOUNTAIN.

37. SUR LE DOURO.
    ON THE DOURO.

38. VENDANGES PRÈS DE VILA NOVA DE FAMILIÇÃO.
    WINE HARVESTING NEAR VILA NOVA DE FAMILIÇÃO.

39. PRÈS DE BARCELOS
NEAR BARCELOS

CHAPTER II

Coimbra and its Surroundings

BETWEEN the Oporto and Lisbon districts lie the three provinces of Beira Alta (capital Viseu), Beira Baixa (capital Castelo Branco) and Beira Litoral (capital Coimbra). Viseu awaits us with the paintings of Grão Vasco, and Coimbra with its churches and museum and the valley of the Mondego where every year poetry and art outlive the green fields and the flowers. Nowhere else perhaps does the landscape compose such a graceful harmony of line and colour. Yet in places a rough note breaks in on the general charm, for the surface enchantment cannot hide the two basic elements of the geography of Portugal: the skeleton of mountains which, once laid bare, stands revealed in all its rugged strength; and the sea fringed, as at Aveiro, with its picturesque coastline. More than any other part of the country, this central region exhales a refined and sober melancholy: to the purity of its air and the variegated charm of its scenery it adds the attraction of its artistic treasures and the character of its inhabitants.

Whether one comes from Oporto or from Lisbon, a tour of the Beiras must be arranged as a lover's approach to Coimbra, that cheerful and vivacious town, the capital of the old kingdom and, thanks to its university, the chosen seat of learning. The best way to appreciate the charm of Coimbra is, in my opinion, to take the route leading from the Spanish frontier. You pass through Valladolid and Salamanca, resting-places in the immense desert. Few are the travellers who penetrate beyond this latter town: yet there is a wealth of wonderful scenery to be admired along the 50 miles of road between Salamanca and Ciudad Rodrigo. The horizon recedes endlessly above the fresh countryside, nothing dims the brightness of the sky. Flocks of sheep roam peacefully across the heath; two storks alight on the banks of a lake, and fly away as you approach. We reach the outer suburbs of Ciudad Rodrigo; but this heroic city, the scene of so many battles, will be better appreciated if viewed from the opposite side. If we look back on it from the frontier, we see the ring of fortifications, Henry II's castle and the cathedral, surrounded by narrow streets and emblazoned palaces. A new road leads straight to the frontier: the old and more picturesque road wound its way through the narrow and devious streets of little-known villages apparently untouched by the hand of time. At last we reach Fuentes de Oñoro, the last town in Spain, and Vilar Formoso, the first in Portugal. We need not linger over the obvious and striking contrast between the neatness of Vilar and the squalor of the villages we have left behind. More interesting are the progressive change of scenery and the gradual appearance of details which tell us we are in Portugal. There are the same stretches of country as surrounded us on the way from Ciudad Rodrigo; but suddenly on our right, perched on its peak, appears Castelo Bom, dazzling white as it towers over part of the valley. Step by step the scenery changes. The broad rocky mountains are clothed in indefinable, ambiguous colours, neither grey nor beige, which the April trees seem striving to imitate; but the buds and blossoms on the slopes lend a human touch to their powerful austerity, differentiating them from certain regions of Castile. The sides of the valleys are strewn with clumps of pines, the distant fields melt gradually into the heights: a new kind of peace steals over us as our eyes distinguish the golden-yellow of the flowers, the greyish tints of the rocks and the lavender-blue of the sky.

Guarda, whose origins go back to Roman times, has the same situation and function in Portugal as Ciudad Rodrigo in Spain. Lying at a height of 3,408 feet, it dominates the whole countryside and controls its defence system. The road grows steeper as we approach, and there is a stiff climb to the Largo Luis de Camoes, the centre of the town. The lower part is lined with arcaded houses, while in the background up above rises the north façade of the cathedral, which, like the town itself, is at once rural and lively, vigorous and fresh. The side façade, looking on the square, with its pinnacles and flying-buttresses whose balustrading reminds us of Batalha, prepares the way for the robust elegance of the main façade with its two massive towers framing the portal and rose-window. The church was begun about 1390, and although giving an impression of unity is actually a mixture of two styles. The choir, transept and outside flying-buttresses are Gothic, the naves and the portal of the main façade are the work of the Manueline architect Boytac, disclosing here and there in their ornamentation the Cross of the Order of Christ, rope-twists and star-spangled vaults. The retable of the high altar is the work of Jean de Rouen and his school. It has been said, rather unkindly, of this retable that 'by its lack of unity in design and consistency in execution it belongs to the artist's decadent period, when his production was beginning to show signs of commercialization' (1550–1553). The delicate carving of the several tiers depicting the life of Christ appears, no doubt, a little fragile in comparison with the vigorous architecture of the vaults, but the retable as a whole provides the eye with a worthy termination to the noble perspective of the nave. The surroundings of the cathedral and of the Largo Luis de Camoes are crowded with narrow streets containing a number of emblazoned houses: here we encounter the ageless Portugal of tradition—women dressed in black, ancient houses and old smoke-stained shops. The main street leads to the modern avenues with their blocks of smart flats looking out over the mountains. Thus we can pass at almost one step from the most sumptuous modern building to the house where King Diniz spent his honeymoon, or to the two adjacent houses where King John entertained his mistress Inez, whose bastard son founded the house of Braganza.

Not far off are the Torre dos Ferreiros, a relic of the ancient wall, and the old bishop's palace, now part barracks part museum, with a Renaissance cloister hidden behind its seventeenth-century façade.

Greatly to be preferred to all these buildings, either too old or too new, is the ravishing Misericordia church. This is like an exquisite *salon* adorned for our entertainment by some boudoir saint. It is built and decorated in the Baroque style, in the taste displayed by so many other Portuguese churches, all of which have certain common characteristics: limewashed outer walls, either white in the Colonial style, or blue and pink and green like a confectioner's; granite frames to doors and windows; a profusion of carved and gilded woodwork inside. In the Misericordia church this riot of colour, of sinuous line and ornamentation, is allied to an astonishing felicity and sureness of touch. The nave is surmounted by a blue wooden cradle-vault. The high altar blazes with gold. Equally dazzling are the four side-altars rhythmically spaced like the steps of a dance. Everywhere there are contorted pediments, affected angels and pillars of pink or green imitation marble. Confronting each other are two small pulpits, and the statues on their sounding-boards seem to pour forth their song like a pair of aristocratic opera stars. Here religious emotion is compounded of an affectionate elegance, a delicate joy of life and thanksgiving for that joy . . . it is no trouble to practise a care-free religion in this cool and natural atmosphere, the blessed gift of the gods.

Before leaving Guarda, with the memory of the exquisite Misericordia church fresh in mind, it might seem appropriate to compare the town to Spanish Avila, since a high altitude and a warlike history are common to both. Nevertheless, the comparison must not be pressed too far. Avila, in fact, is a warrior town girt with ramparts and towers, through whose streets lined with frowning palaces the wind from the Meseta stirs memories of the mystical heroism of St Teresa. Guarda has practically nothing left of its walls, and the only memories evoked in the streets are those of country virtues and bravery in war.

The road to the south leads to Castelo Branco. Little of interest is to be found in the ruins of the castle, the old enciente, the small picture-collection in the museum, which includes a *St Anthony* attributed to Francisco Henriques. In the terraced gardens of the bishop's palace there is a famous staircase of statues representing the Kings of Portugal; otherwise the town is of no importance from an artistic point of view and we should do better to push on to Viseu, pausing on the way in the Serra da Estrêla.

This range, containing the highest peaks and the most interesting mountains in Portugal, runs out from the angle formed by the roads from Celorico da Beira to Guarda and from Guarda to Covilha. Its wonderful valleys have had a universal appeal: poets have always loved the limpid beauty of its rock-water and the tranquil silence of its underwoods; shepherds in their broad felt hats and heavy woollen cloaks tend their flocks of sheep and goats, there are winter sports for the ski-runner and *pousadas* (inns) for the tourist, while the engineers are busy constructing their hydro-electric works. There are wonderful views such as that from the Malhão da Estrêla, the highest peak in Portugal. One may stop to admire some venerable church or Calvary, or dream away the hours before the rocks of the Penhas Douradas and the Cântaro Magro or lakes like the Lagoa Comprida.

From Guarda to Viseu the road opens up one after another superb view of the mountains. Every now and then a peasant woman passes on the side of the road, dressed in black and walking with time-honoured dignity. She holds her head erect under the swaying basket, which looks as if it would fall off at any moment, and carries in a voluminous shawl a baby whose tiny body is scarcely to be distinguished from its wrappings. And the landscape is as delightful as its inhabitants. Among the box-trees bordering the road, gay pools of flowers sparkle in the sunshine. Farther on, the houses come into view, the small window-panes shimmering in the noonday glare and surrounded by a versatile chequer-work of blue, pink and white. Once past Celorico da Beira and its ruined castle we are left alone once more to the beauties of nature.

The meadows on either side of the river at the bottom of the valley are carpeted with flowers—the common buttercup or daisy. The pleasant prospect is like a pastoral poem or a painting whose appeal derives from charm rather than from any compelling beauty: yet side by side with this pastoral scene stand the barren mountains, and scattered boulders bear witness to the ubiquitous subsoil of rock beneath.

Viseu remains in the memory of the hurried visitor as the show town of Portugal: busy shopping streets, shady gardens and squares bursting with flowers, brightly painted old houses with their coats of arms on the walls. The town claims several sons famous in history, such as Viriathus, commemorated by a statue by Benlliure, although it is not certain that he ever lived in these parts; and Roderick the last king of the Goths, whose sepulchre is in the church of São Pedro de Feital. The hanging staircase of the Seminario is a mere curiosity: the unique show-pieces of Viseu are the cathedral and the Grão Vasco Museum.

Coimbra and its Surroundings

We climb the steep streets, dominated by the graceful colonnade which stands on its massive foundation next to the metropolitan church, and push our way through the stalls of the open-air shoe-market. At the top, surrounding the Cathedral Square, we find the Misericordia, whose granite severity is softened by the Baroque curves of the doors and windows; the old seminary now occupied by a library and museum; and finally the cathedral itself. The square breathes an atmosphere of harmonious, cloistral calm, and the severity of the buildings is warmed by the soft midday sun. The noble but somewhat heavy façade of the cathedral (the towers are Romanesque and the doorway seventeenth century) and the bareness of the old seminary are relieved by the graceful proportions of the hospital and the pillars of the colonnade, open to the town and the sky: the stonework is uniform in colour and design.

In any case, the interior of the cathedral is a miracle of lightness. On the twelfth-century columns of the nave rests a Manueline vaulted roof with thick knotted cable groining, John II's pelican and Afonso V's mill-wheel inscribed with the word 'Never'. The cloister dates from the middle of the sixteenth century. There is a remarkable collection of relics and ornaments, including some Limoges chased enamel reliquaries and a delectable *presepio* or crib surrounded by a crowd which admirably conjures up the traditional Nativity scene.

On the square to the left a door next to the cathedral opens to admit us to the museum, and as we pass from one building to the other we notice the identical atmosphere and the same soft gleam of stone. Here is the ideal place for a collection of pictures painted for or inspired by the church, in whose shadow they have now found shelter. The collection provides a complete and accurate conspectus of art in Viseu during the first decades of the sixteenth century. They appeal not only to our aesthetic sense but to our feeling for everyday life: not far from the museum lived the men whose works we admire, many of which have long adorned the cathedral for which they were painted; for Viseu at that time was a notable art-centre.

Vasco Fernandes, the Grão Vasco, has a special room in the gallery to himself hung with five of his finest paintings. *St Peter* shows the saint seated on a monumental throne; he looks grave and a little sad, as if weighed down by his responsibility as Pope, the teacher of the one true Faith. We see an aged man, loaded with magnificent vestments which scarcely avail to hide the plebeian origin betrayed by his pronounced features and sturdy build: even the Early Renaissance style can do little to lighten the picture's heavy atmosphere. *Calvary* shows a pathetic buffeted Christ, with landscape and figures swept by the same contrary winds: the savagery with which the Crucifixion is depicted contrasts with the refined treatment of the draperies of the Virgin and her companions. *St Sebastian, The Baptism of Christ* and *Pentecost* are paintings filled with a shuddering tortured spirituality. Art in Viseu was not confined to the masterpieces of Grão Vasco: the great retable of the cathedral, now in the museum, was sculpted about the year 1505. This work was for a long time mistakenly attributed to Francisco Henriques or to Grão Vasco himself. Its unknown author displays his originality in the lyrical emotion of *Calvary, The Garden of Olives* and *The Adoration of the Magi* with its tossing drapery, contrasted forms, and landscape filled with a dim pathos. After Grão Vasco, the principal painter of Viseu was Gaspar Vaz: his *Christ in the House of Martha* combines genuine feeling with a refined and picturesque treatment of the setting.

On leaving Viseu we proceed towards São Pedro do Sul. Along the mountain roads the slender trunks and lofty branches of the pines stand out against a sky of limpid blue. We are travelling west, towards the sea, through an unbroken stretch of magnificent scenery. The mountain-sides slope up in tiers of every shade of green, the song of the birds rises amid the pungent perfume of the flowers, the houses come into view in their dainty setting of clustering plants.

At the mouth of the Vouga the coastal district of Aveiro has a character of its own, due to its delta 30 miles long by 5 miles broad. A mysterious haze floats above this land of lagoons and canals and salt-marshes, saturated by the sea and at the same time isolated by the sand-dunes thrown up by the Atlantic. In the vaporous twilight land and sea and sky melt into one like the Dutch polders; the salt-mounds sparkle in the sun, and in the total silence the humidity of the atmosphere imparts a musical vibration to the slightest shock. A dazzling multi-coloured procession of barges, laden with fish, rushes, reeds and salt advances steadily with no other sound but the water rippling at their bows as they spread their white or red sails against the green stretches of the coast, while the mist swallows the swan-necks of their prows and sterns and the crescents of their hulls.

While the country reminds us of Holland, its inhabitants are of Phoenician type, descendants probably of sailors settled in the district for centuries past. The fishermen live on the dunes in huts perched on wooden piles. To go for a sail with them is an unforgettable experience: their parti-coloured boats carry us to a world which is no longer either land or river, and will soon become the sea. . . .

The fields, we observe, are encroaching on the waters. Ovar was once a port, and still contains a few picturesque fishermen's houses.

The principal attraction of Aveiro is the convent (now a museum) of the Princess Santa Joãna, daughter of Afonso V, who spent her life there as a nun from 1475 to 1489. The church—the wonderful Church of Jesus—is smothered in carved and gilded wood. The pillars are wrought like gold-plate, the rosettes project and intersect in an overlapping combination like a poet's dream of treasure-trove. The round roof is studded with stars. Our bewildered eyes end by seeing nothing but gold and more gold, wrought and re-wrought, gilt and re-gilt—a gorgeous cope teeming with all the flora of the Indies, laid up in homage in the House of God.

The saint lies in her marble marquetry tomb in the lower choir. The cloister, the refectory and the small adjacent rooms are decorated with charming carved woodwork, full of the peaceful memory of the nuns. The perfume of flowers mingles with the musical breezes of the cloister; a delightful little reading-cell opens out of the refectory; the small side-rooms contain a number of statues and tombs. The Casa do Lavor, the room where the saint died, was converted in the eighteenth century into a chapel blazing with gold.

The museum houses a collection of priceless treasures. The famous portrait of Afonso V's daughter is generally attributed to the school of

Nuno Gonçalves. A lasting impression is made by the hard features, the lines of the lips and chin, the face of youth devoured by sanctity, the mouth and eyes expressive of a mysterious disdain. We enter a kind of rustic fairyland crowded with retables and innocent saints, a delightful world created by the faith of a pious peasantry. St Anselm and the Infant Jesus are wrapped in real sheets: the Holy Family modelled in clay wear amusing three-cornered hats, and their blue and gold robes are spangled with all the flowers of the field.

It is now time to push on to Coimbra: whichever road we take, that wonderful city awaits us, though there are many beauty-spots and fine works of art to be inspected on the way. On market-day the villagers file past on their way to town, the women as usual walking barefoot and carrying bundles on their heads. Wagons with high wicker sides roll by on huge painted wheels, drawn by oxen under their carved yoke.

Along the coast we pass through Ilhavo, home of sailors and fishermen, whose museum has a fine collection of porcelain and glass from the factory at Vista Alegre near by. Figueira da Foz offers a famous beach. Montemor-o-Velho, by the green banks of the Mondego, has some attractive old churches and a recumbent effigy of Diogo de Azambuja the Navigator by Diogo Pires-o-Moço.

Inland we come upon the soft limestone quarries of Ança which supplied the Renaissance sculptors of Coimbra and the surrounding district. Cantanhede, and particularly Varziela with its retable by Jean de Rouen, offer a foretaste of the artistic treasures of Coimbra. Lastly, a few miles from the city, hidden in the fields at the end of a rough lane, stands the astonishing pile of the ancient Hieronymite convent of São Marcos. This contains fifteenth- and sixteenth-century tombs of the da Silva and Meneses families, a high altar retable by Nicolas Chanterène (about 1523) and a ravishing Renaissance chapel of the Magi, built of stone as white as the Mondego countryside.

Coimbra is a city to be admired as a whole, and studied carefully before plunging into its streets. On the left bank of the Mondego a rough path climbs to the new convent of Santa Clara and to the green ranches just outside the built-up area. Behind the river stretches the station quarter:

then, after climbing the hill, we meet the grey and white jumble of streets in the old town, with the noble mass of the Romanesque cathedral standing out like the iron crown of a warrior king. Still higher up we catch sight of the Machado de Castro Museum, with the spotless arches of its arcade outlined against the pure sky; then come the buildings and tower of the old university, and the huge dazzling blocks of the new. All around on the other hills are spread villas embowered in green, and the public gardens. The innumerable flower-beds shaded by trees add an almost Florentine delicacy to the scene, and in the distance the splashes of blue, pink and green houses, themselves like larger flowers, compose a picture of perpetual spring.

The old convent was founded on the river bank by the Holy Queen, St Isabella, the wife of King Diniz. After it was flooded, the nuns removed to the vast and magnificent new convent of Santa Clara on the hill, built in the seventeenth century. In the chapel stands the statue of the foundress by Teixera Lopes, over a tomb of glass and chased silver (1614). Of far greater merit are the two polychrome Gothic stone tombs at the foot of the nave, and the original tomb of the queen in the nuns' choir. She lies on a coffer of Flamboyant design, her head beneath a canopy, watched over by angels.

The Mondego, which lends such beauty to the district and evokes such poetical memories, has inflicted great damage to its banks through flooding. It has gradually encroached on and silted up the old convent of Santa Clara. The massive bulk of the early fourteenth-century church is supported by sturdy buttresses: it retains, in spite of its date, that flavour of Romanesque so frequently met with in the High Gothic period in Portugal. The convent once contained many art treasures: among the sculptures were the admirable tomb of the foundress erected in 1330 and now in the new convent, and a Christ in the Sepulchre lying above the sleeping soldiers, now in the museum. In the museum are also to be seen, among the paintings, the fragments of the retable depicting the Passion, by Quentin Metsys; and a number of objects of truly feminine appeal, such as the reliquary of the True Cross and the necklace belonging to the queen, relics which evoke the fragile charm of a delicate piety.

The memory of another woman comes to mind, no heroic saint but a tragic lover. It was on this spot that Inez de Castro was murdered.

How difficult it is to conjure up sanctity, love and death in their original setting! The church belongs to a very different world, and its surroundings, through which the road to Lisbon runs, are mean and noisy. The Mondego has left nothing of the convent but the flooded church below the level of the soil. Embedded in shabby houses, surrounded by featureless fields and abandoned, not to the tranquil oblivion of the open country but to the poignant ugliness of suburbia, the church is now nothing more than a reservoir on which you can go for a row. One imagines the oars striking the sea-green water under the ancient vaults, and pictures the sky—the only friend whose beauty has never been grudged—gazing through the gaping windows into the ice-cold church.

Higher upstream the farms, such as the Quinta das Canas and the Quinta das Lágrimas, have wonderful gardens and a superb view. In the Quinta das Lágrimas, at the end of a long avenue shaded by exotic trees, is set the Fountain of the Loves, celebrated by Camoëns. Here, according to legend, Inez was murdered, meeting her death in a fit setting of murmuring leaves and rustling waters.

We cross the Mondego, and are swallowed up immediately in the noise and bustle of Coimbra. To us Coimbra is an intellectual centre, but to the peasants who crowd in from the surrounding country it is merely a large town where they can sell their produce and do their shopping, and their presence lends to some of the streets the aspect of a market town. The students in their short black cassocks and voluminous black cloaks can be classified by the colour of the ribbons attached to their satchels, seniority being indicated by the length of the ribbons: the *quemada das bilas*, the bonfire of the ribbons, is the occasion for a grand celebration.

Between the avenue which runs along the river to the station, and the Rua Ferreira Borges at the foot of the hill on which the old town stands, we must step aside into the narrow streets pervaded by a strong smell of stale and rancid butter. The steep pavements are cluttered with untidy stalls; the indefatigable peasant women, with the inevitable basket balanced on their heads, patter by on their bare and dirty feet; the air is filled with the stench of invisible fish. The eighteenth-century church of São Bartolomeu is of less interest than the church of São Tiago with its Romanesque portals—a reminder of the days when the old cathedral was surrounded by churches, when Coimbra was a centre of medieval art.

At the Renaissance there was a second wave of building, which is first encountered in the monastery of Santa Cruz. This building, at the foot of the hill containing the old quarters, is one of the finest in Portugal. It was founded by Afonso I and rebuilt at the beginning of the sixteenth century by King Manuel, who commissioned Boytac to carry out the work of restoration (1508–1513). Cristovão de Figueiredo and, in particular, Nicolas Chanterène and his school worked on the decoration. The main façade, blackened by time but with occasional long strips where the soft stone shows through like scars, carries on the noble lines of the doorway and the window above; the general design was laid down by Diogo de Castilho in 1523, the statues are the work of Chanterène. The latter was also responsible for the pulpit in the nave (1521), which in the purity of its carving resembles a piece of plate or the enlargement of the handle of some precious chalice or crozier: from its bed we seem to see springing a magnificent slender tree, growing on the steps of the Virgin's heavenly throne.

In the choir, the recumbent effigies of Afonso Henriques and Sancho I are from the hand of the same artist (1518–1521), who is also credited with some of the statues in the niches. The retable of the high altar was once adorned with a polyptych by Cristovão de Figueiredo, the fragments of which are now in the museum and the sacristy of the monastery. The spacious sacristy, built by Pedro Numes Tinocco in 1640, is richly decorated beneath its cradle-vault, and contains some notable *azulejos* and paintings: among the latter the most impressive are a *Crucifixion* from the high altar and an *Ecce Homo*, both by Cristovão de Figueiredo, and two medallions by Vasco Fernandes.

The *Cloister of Silence* is Manueline, and contains a graceful fountain: to Chanterène once more are ascribed the bas-reliefs inspired by engravings of Albrecht Dürer's *Passion*. In the monks' choir above the main entrance of the church, the most pleasing stalls are those carved not by Machim (1512) or the French artist François Lorette (1531) but by João Aleman: these, though somewhat heavy in the German style, are remarkable for their Manueline motifs, their fantastic representation of town scenes, and the gaiety of their gilt statues.

To the left of the Santa Cruz Monastery is the 'Jardim da Manga', which John III is said to have designed on his sleeve. This was formerly a cloister built by Jean de Rouen: in the middle is a delightful building made up of four chapels joined by arches to a central dome (1533): the perfect harmony of the curves is as thrilling as a piece of music, and the lines of the arches have the purity of a fountain.

The Avenida Sa da Bandeira winds round the hillside to the summit and the old town. We may prefer to climb the precipitous streets which lead to the top of the hill. After a glance at the roof of the Arco de Almedina, one of the city's oldest fortified gates, we may pay a visit to the Manueline palace of Sub-Ripas and the Colegio da Misericordia, whose noble cloister resembles that of the Felipes in Tomar. The narrow, steep and winding streets are a challenge to the virtuosity of the cyclists who rush up and down them with incredible skill, without in the least disturbing the leisurely progress of the old women, who remain as indifferent to the clamour of the cyclists as to the inexpressibly sweet song of the birds nesting in the cathedral.

We are now in sight of the old cathedral, or Sé Velha. Sturdy and battlemented, graceful owing to the cleanness of its lines, and owing its lightness to the circumstance of being built on a slope, it stands out from the hillside against the sky. It is the most beautiful Romanesque church in Portugal, as Santa Cruz is unique of its kind.

Its architecture and decoration remind one at the same time of the churches of Auvergne, of the French Renaissance, and of Flanders at the end of the Middle Ages. It was built by the master-builders Robert and Bernard about the years 1160–1170. The geometric ornamentation of the west door belongs to this period, and provides a striking contrast with the north *porta especiosa*. This last, dating from about 1530, is probably the work of Nicolas Chanterène, and is merely the excuse for a ravishing triple-tiered display of exquisite carving, comprising medallions, arabesques, niches, pilasters and columns with flowered capitals. Inside the church the semicircular cradle—or groined vaults—terminate in a blaze of polychrome woodwork and sharp lines, smothered in a riot of ornament. The high altar is remarkable for a retable made by Olivier de Bruges and Jean de Gand for Bishop Jorge d'Almeida (1498-1508). On the other hand, the chapel of the Blessed Sacrament is pure Renaissance in style, with a double tier of statues of the apostles by Tomé Velho standing in niches inlaid with shells. The decoration of the Manueline baptismal fonts is a little heavy, but redeemed by a touch of fantasy. The adjoining late thirteenth-century cloister has a fine display of capitals.

Continuing our uphill climb past the Romanesque church of San Salvador, we reach the Machado de Castro Museum in the old Episcopal Palace on the top of the hill: the building, in the Renaissance style, is attributed to Filippo Terzi. On entering the *patio* we are immediately struck by the coolness of the courtyard, the brilliance of the walls and the exquisitely proportioned arcade which, silhouetted against the sky, enchants the eye with a glorious view of the city. As we advance through the various rooms we can enjoy the view as well as the treasures of art. A tranquil beauty pervades everything, a happy combination of city, art and flowers.

The museum contains some of the treasures from the old cathedral and monasteries of the city—Santa Clara, Santa Cruz, Celas—as well as from the surrounding countryside. Thus it both represents Coimbra's two golden centuries of art—the wonderful capitals of the Romanesque period, and the Renaissance sculpture by French artists gleaming white against the green valleys of the Mondego—and also demonstrates the close connection between Flemish and Portuguese painting.

The greatest number of exhibits come from the convent of Santa Clara. On the volets of a large fifteenth-century triptych we see a *Garden of Olives* and a *Descent from the Cross*, with the disciples and onlookers standing in attitudes taut with grief: on the centre panel St Clara, with averted eyes and custodial in hand, drives away the Saracens; she moves in a dream-world of passionate prayer. Then there are the fragments of the retable of Quentin Metsys' *Passion* bought in Antwerp for King Manuel by his agent Silvestre Nunez and presented to the convent: the Virgin, her face ravaged with grief, her hands crossed over her heart, draped from head to foot in a flowing gold-bordered veil; a *Flagellation* and an *Ecce Homo* with faces dumbfounded with grief or contorted with bestial hate. There is a *Deposition from the Cross* by the Master of the Prodigal Son (possibly a native of Antwerp in the first half of the sixteenth century) in which the wasted faces seem as though blurred with agony. From the convent of Santa Cruz come the tau-cross of the prior (by a brief of 1153 Pope Anastasius IV had granted the superiors of the convent the use of the pontifical insignia) and two fragments of the high altar retable painted by Cristovão de Figueiredo: *The Finding of the True Cross by St Helena* and *The Emperor Heraclius on horseback, bearing in triumph the newly rediscovered Cross of the Crucifixion*. From the convent in Celas, which must also have contained many treasures, comes a sixteenth-century *Magdalen*, part of a polyptych: her long golden hair covers her naked body as she is wafted to heaven by the angels. The mannered and archaizing Master of Celas, obviously Flemish and possibly also from Antwerp, is one of the most engaging artists represented in the museum. He is at the same time affected and poetical, tender-hearted and pathetic, addicted to elaborate compositions, stately draperies and care-worn faces: his *Nativity* and his composite portrait of John the Baptist and St Philip are suffused with solemn emotion; in his *Entombment* he puts forth all his skill without obscuring the anguish of the scene. The adjoining *Crucifixion* shows the influence of van Orley.

There is much else to claim our attention, for the Machado de Castro Museum is second only in importance to Lisbon's Museum of Ancient Art. There is a remarkable *Christ appearing to the Virgin* by a painter of the school of Cristovão de Figueiredo: the Mother bends with trembling joy before the Redeemer, who, with a gesture of love and respect, raises the bowed body. Another painting by Andriaen Isenbrandt shows an exquisite Virgin with the Child resting His chin on His hand.

Among the never-to-be-forgotten sculptures is a black wooden Christ, the head bowed beneath the burden of human misery, the brow girt with the crown of thorns, the still curling hair falling to the shoulders. Of the bas-reliefs of Jean de Rouen's 'Jardim da Manga' we have *The Temptation of St Anthony* and *The Repentance of St Jerome*. By the same artist is a *Virgin and Child*, the statue of a rosy-cheeked, neatly dressed peasant girl, her waist tightly encircled in a full apron-like skirt. We may perhaps attribute to Chanterène another Virgin, listening on her knees in modest acceptance to the words of Gabriel. The sharp features of a Manueline angel by Diogo Pires-o-Moço are stamped with the solemn happiness of a heavenly courtier: in his graceful modesty he might be a squire bearing the arms of his Lord. In contrast with the talent displayed in these charming and competent paintings, Hodart's *Apostles* bears the stamp of genius in the sweep and vigour of its passionate inspiration.

The museum possesses a fine collection of textiles, pottery and church vessels. The silver-gilt chalice by Geda Menendiz (1152) is a most beautiful example of the Romanesque period. The sixteenth-century chalices are purely Portuguese, Gothic in the Flamboyant carved handles, but with cups overflowing with luxuriant leaf-work.

Compared with these splendid collections there is little to detain us in the heavy, lifeless new cathedral. All around work is going on to level the summit which formerly housed one of the quarters of the old city, and to clear the space needed for the modern buildings of the university. These buildings, most of which are already built and in use, contrast strangely in their stark brilliance with the delicate contours of the surrounding country: nevertheless their spacious simplicity is in harmony with the old buildings, which we enter by the Porta Ferrea (1634).

The university has more than once been moved from Lisbon to Coimbra, and was formerly housed in the convent of Santa Cruz before being installed, with the requisite alterations and extensions, in the royal palace which is its present home. Thus the noble Paço das Escolas, with its snow-white buildings gleaming in the blinding sun, is surrounded on three sides by buildings of different dates. The Manueline chapel is by Marcos Pires; its *azulejos* date from the seventeenth century, as does the Sala dos Capelos, under whose magnificent coffered ceiling the undergraduates take their degrees. Near the broad walk of the Via Latina an eighteenth-century tower makes a pleasant break in the horizontal lines of the courtyard. Most impressive of all is the Library (1716–1723), an ostentatious building crammed with marbles and costly woodwork and innumerable ornaments. Yet this exuberant decoration never spoils the architectural proportions, nor does the eye ever lose itself under the roofs festooned with branches like those which, in far-away Brazil, arch over the unexplored rivers. It is a sight to dazzle and overwhelm, for nowhere in all this riot of decoration is it possible to detect a single inch of unnecessary gilding. . . . The galleries running round the walls above our shoulders seem as far off and imponderable as the sky itself: it is as if a mild springtime had caused all the golden fruits of the lost paradise to bloom again. Outside in the Paço das Escolas, scarcely more spacious than the Library itself, on the fourth side of the courtyard, we can lean over the most beautiful balcony ever dreamt of by human architect. It looks towards the unruffled peace of the mountain and the friendly brightness of the sky. The near-by gardens are full of the perfume of flowers, the narrow streets hurry down the hillside, the Mondego winds slowly between the meadows and the rocks. Lucky are the pupils who are privileged to pursue their studies in this rarefied atmosphere, in this university lying ever open to the beauties of nature and of art.

Near the botanic gardens the Roman aqueduct, rebuilt at the Renaissance and crowned with a delightful little chapel dedicated to St Sebastian, strides across the landscape like a stone giant. Still higher up, the gardens continue towards Celas, where we can see some storied capitals, a Chanterène door and some altars by Jean de Rouen. Finally, on the top of the hill, we come to Santo Antonio dos Olivais with its memories of St Anthony of Padua. Here our climb ends on the terrace which runs round the church, with a view on three sides of a broad undulating stretch of country whose belts of shadow or sunshine are carpeted with unassuming or dazzling flowers. For the buildings of Coimbra breathe the very poetry of the countryside, where the shrill song of the crickets blends with the many-tinted fields and woods and the penetrating perfume of invincible flowers.

Equally attractive are the environs of the city. Green gardens lap the

Coimbra and its Surroundings

near-by watering-place of Luso. Upstream from Coimbra the valley of the Mondego is narrow, rocky and winding, dominated by Penacova, which towers above in a setting worthy of Victor Hugo's *Les Burgraves*. An unexpected and most amusing feature of Bussaco is its imitation Manueline luxury hotel, formerly a palace, which looks as if it had been built with toy bricks by a precocious child in parody of Belem and Tomar. The forest surrounding and covering the promontory contains many unique species, and the belvedere at Cruz Alta floats like a buoy in the limitless sea of hills and forests and villages. It is as if, at the foot of a rainbow, some whim of the Creator had suddenly re-created the whole world and decked it with its finest spring flowers.

GUARDA.

TERRASSE DE LA CATHÉDRALE.
THE CATHEDRAL TERRACE.

. CASTELO-BRANCO.
RDINS DE L'ANCIEN PALAIS ÉPISCOPAL.
ARDENS OF THE OLD EPISCOPAL PALACE.

42. VISEU.
LA MISERICORDIA.
THE MISERICORDIA.

43.
PRÈS D'AVEIRO.
NEAR AVEIRO.

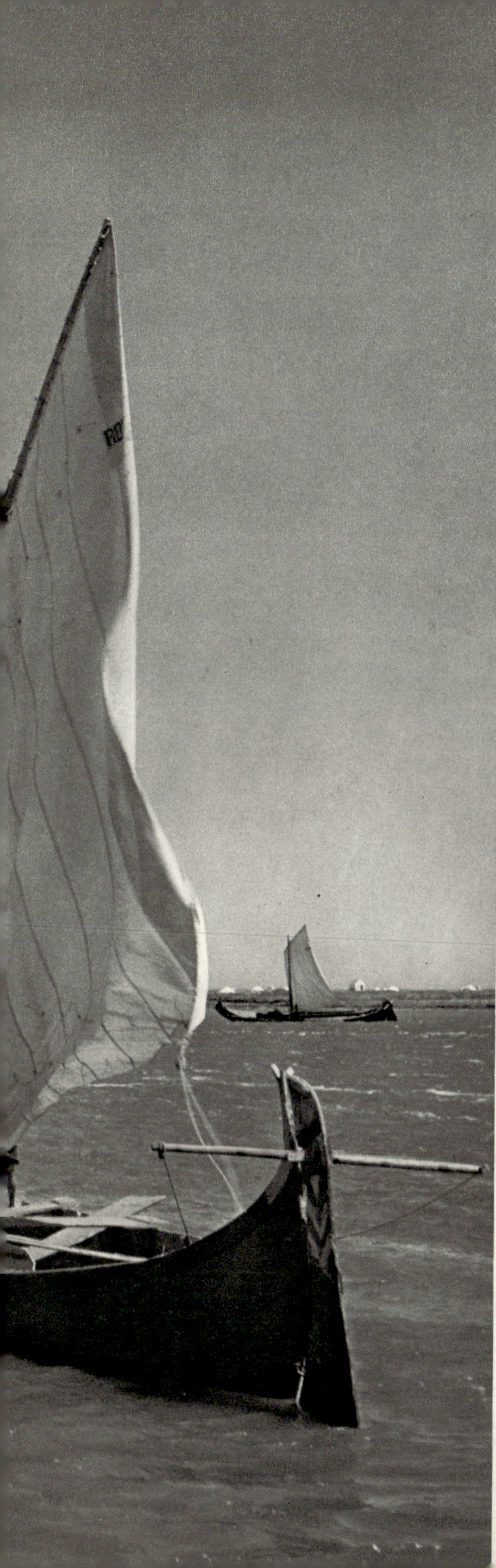

44-45-46. AVEIRO.
MOLICEIROS SUR LA RIA.
MOLICEIROS ON THE RIA.

COIMBRA.

47. VUE SUR LA CATHÉDRALE.
    VIEW ONTO THE CATHEDRAL.

48. PATIO DU MUSÉE MACHADO DE CASTRO.
    PATIO OF THE MACHADO DE CASTRO MUSEUM.

COIMBRA.
L'UNIVERSITÉ.
THE UNIVERSITY.

49. LA NOUVELLE UNIVERSITÉ VUE DE LA PORTA FERREA.
    THE NEW UNIVERSITY SEEN FROM THE PORTA FERREA.

50. LA VIA LATINA.
    THE VIA LATINA.

COIMBRA.

1. PLAFOND DE LA BIBLIOTHÈQUE DE L'UNIVERSITÉ.
   CEILING OF THE LIBRARY OF THE UNIVERSITY.

2. MONASTÈRE DE SANTA CRUZ. CHAIRE DE NICOLAS CHANTERÈNE.
   THE MONASTERY OF SANTA CRUZ. PULPIT OF NICHOLAS CHANTERÈNE.

53. VERS LA CATHÉDRALE.
TOWARDS THE CATHEDRAL.

54. PORTE DU PALACIO SUB-RIPAS.
DOOR OF THE PALACIO SUB-RIPAS.

COIMBRA.

55.
MUSÉE MACHADO DE CASTRO. LE CHRIST NOIR.
THE MACHADO DE CASTRO MUSEUM. THE BLACK CHRIST.

56.
ANCIEN COUVENT SANTA CLARA
THE OLD SANTA CLARA CONVEN

57-58-59. COIMBRA.
FÊTES DE LA RAINHA SANTA.
FESTIVAL OF THE RAINHA SANTA.

59

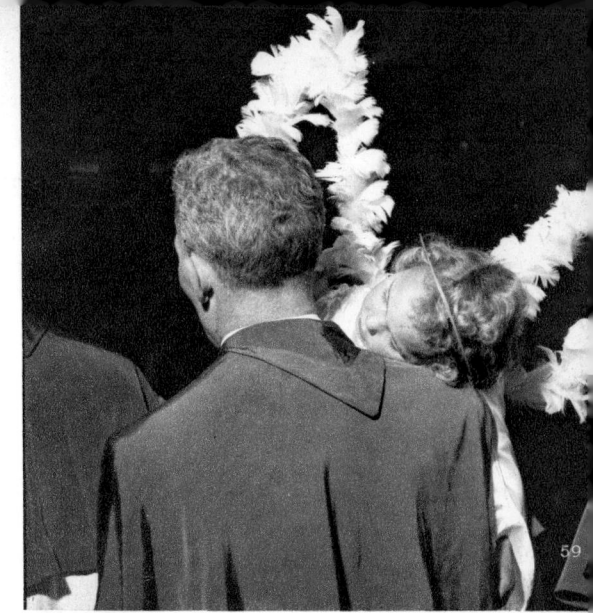

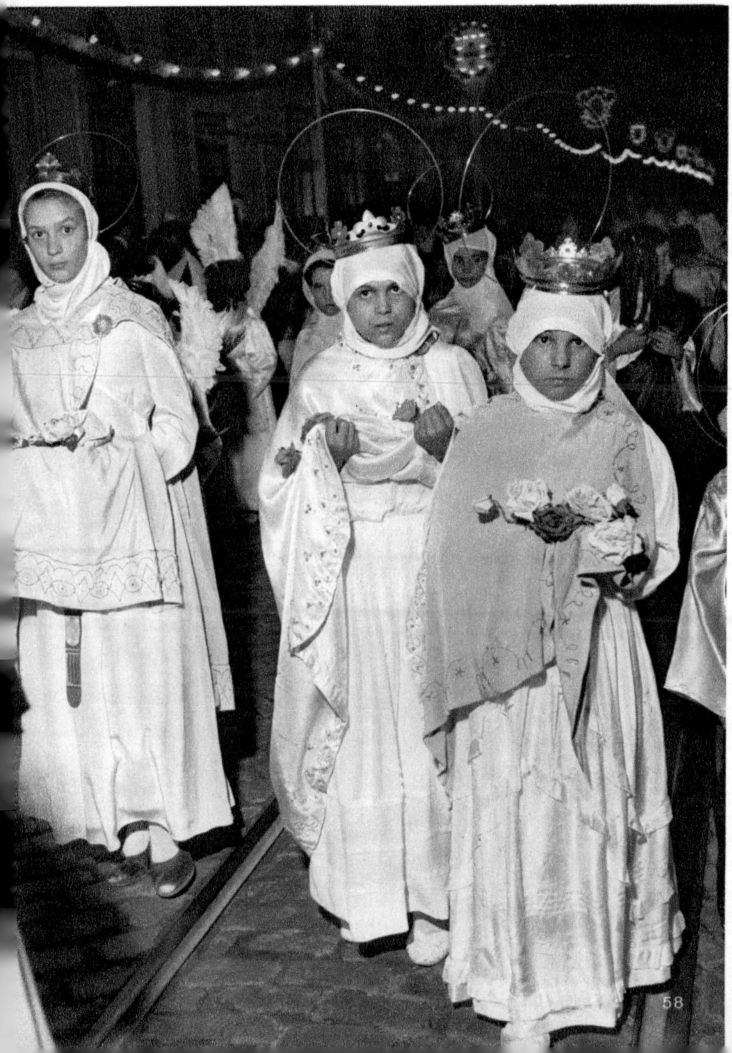
58

CHAPTER III

From Tomar to Nazaré

Our wayward course now takes us through the borders of the provinces of Ribatejo, Beira Litoral and Estremadura. As in the Coimbra region, the same chains of wooded mountains unfold beneath the soft light: the country is just as pleasant, and often just as dry. The spell cast by this narrow belt of land derives from the three or four monasteries or convents which, within this very restricted space, constitute the unique pride of Portugal. Few countries can rival and perhaps none surpass them. Who that has once seen them can ever forget Cistercian Alcobaça or Manueline Tomar or Batalha of Our Lady of Victory? We are fascinated not only by works of art but by typical towns such as the port of Nazaré, which may be considered the most picturesque town in Portugal.

The unique charm of Tomar derives from its Italianate site and buildings, which include the magnificent monastery-fortress. The two-storied aqueduct striding powerfully across the woods and the sky might be Roman: the campaniles of certain churches and the arcades of certain buildings remind us of Italy; the graceful rows of pines which clothe certain of the hills against the skyline of the Serra de Alvelos transport us to Tuscany; and Tuscan, above all, is the spectacle, on the near-by hill crowned with woods and girt with sloping gardens, of the castle-monastery where the Knights of Christ succeeded to the Templars.

The town itself delights us with its parks and tidy streets and ancient churches. On the left bank of the Narvão, in the Alem da Ponte quarter, Santa Maria do Olival, standing detached from its campanile, contains the tombs of the grand masters of the Templars, notably those of Gualdim Pais, who founded the monastery, and of Diogo Pinheiro; in Santa Iria, which has a Renaissance side doorway and choir window, an archway in the Valles Chapel, decorated with heads of Red Indians, discloses a retable in Ança stone representing the Crucifixion, in a style with which

60. BUSSACO
    ESCALIER DE LA FONTE FRIA
    STAIRCASE OF THE FONTE FRIA

we have become familiar in the Mondego valley. Near at hand is the bridge leading to the centre of the town, which provides one of the pleasantest views of Tomar: to the left is a corner house with outer walls of dazzling white; to the right are the lawns and trees of a public garden; in front is the town and the Convent of Christ. Soon we reach the church of St John the Baptist, its façade flanked by a steep-roofed tower: one door is Flamboyant, the other Manueline like the pulpit; the interior is decorated with a series of early sixteenth-century Portuguese paintings.

But the heart of Tomar is the monastery. The imposing conglomeration of buildings is best approached from the north and east: it is defended by ramparts and a keep. The octagonal late twelfth-century church with the circular nave characteristic of the Templars is almost the only example of its kind in Europe. King Manuel in 1510 added a nave by Diogo de Arruda, including a monks' choir loft, and a sacristy underneath, later used as a chapter-house, whose group of three windows provides one of the most wonderful examples of the Manueline style. The Renaissance added several cloisters, one of which, the cloister of the Felipes, is of an unrivalled nobility.

From the foot of the hill, near the old houses and gardens, the road zigzags up to the precinct, entered through the São Tiago gate. Inside the ramparts the groves and flower-beds, the church and its cloisters and the ruined buildings lie side by side, full of a strange poetry compounded of the tranquil heights and mild climate, of glorious memories and shady trees. We enter the church by the south door, whose design and decoration recall the porch at Belem; the stone hangs from the arches like fringes of flowers or stalactites, the innumerable soaring finials seem to breathe. The door was sculpted by João de Castilho in 1515. The original Templars' church, in the vigour and proportion of its design, would have provided a worthy chapter-house for King Arthur and his knights. The decoration added by King Manuel, in spite of its artistic merits, masks more than it enhances the purity of the architecture, and includes some polychrome statues on which Olivier de Gand is known to have worked, and some paintings of the Portuguese school. Of the chapter-house windows, the work of Diogo de Arruda, the most famous is the west window opening on the cloister of Santa Barbara: with the cloister of Belem it represents the highest achievement of Manueline art. This strange work has a mysterious lyrical quality; nor is it surprising that foremost scholars and critics have detected in it influences or parallels deriving from contact with the Indies, with Baroque art, with the flora and the boundless world of the Atlantic, an hypothesis which may receive some support from our knowledge that the Arruda brothers visited Morocco. Considered merely as poetry, such associations are not only possible but even beautiful; but a dispassionate analysis leads to different conclusions. The famous west window, attached to the wall like an enormous jewel by startling ties (one of which consists of the collar still worn by the local cattle) is, taken as whole, a decorative hymn of praise to the cork-oak, the sap and the fertile soil. It may be a poem, but it is invested with an accurate and unexpected symbolism.

The cloister of the Felipes rivals in its perfect proportions the masterpieces of Palladio or Charles V's palace of the Alhambra. The decorative exuberance of Diogo de Arruda here yields place to the classic breadth of style of Diogo de Torralva and Filippo Terzi. Here in this monastery, one of the glories of Portugal's days of independence, Philip II received the crown of Portugal. Many other cloisters are deserving of attention, not perhaps so beautiful as the Felipes, but each with its own special appeal. In the Micha, the monks of old distributed alms; the Cemiterio is Gothic, with arches of an exquisite delicacy; the Santa Barbara and the cloister of the guest quarters distil their tranquil charm. In the arcade of the seminary there is an old Renaissance cell and small chapel; the ancient chapter-house is now a lapidary museum.

A little lower down the hill stands a perfect building, which we may have missed on the way up to Tomar. The church of Santa Maria de Conceição, attributed to Torralva, in the perfection of its balance and proportions and the sobriety of its conception is a masterpiece of classical architecture, as delicate as the over-arching sky: it is a Greek temple set in the woods of Tomar.

The road to the west now ascends through a stretch of barren table-land. As we mount higher, the scenery becomes melancholy, stern and rugged.

Nothing more desolate can be imagined than the heaths of Alburitel or Ourem—an old decaying town whose useless fortress is a reminder of battles long ago—or, above all, Cova da Iria.

It was here, in 1917, that the Virgin appeared to three little shepherds from the village of Fatima—Lucia, Jacinta and Francisco, all three destined to die young or to take the veil. Unfortunately, immense damage was done through the zeal of the first pilgrims in their search for relics, and by their hunger to possess some fragment, however small, from the scene of this miraculous appearance. It became necessary, however regrettable, to put up an enormous esplanade surrounded by a banal church and featureless portico and several cheap hotels. Whereas Lourdes is a town in itself and almost an institution, Fatima remains relatively wild and deserted, and the esplanade, on days when there are no visitors, confronts the blue immensity of the sky like a huge mirror reflecting the footstool of God seated on the heavenly throne. The new Fatima is thus not without a certain feeling of majesty. Huysmans, who was scandalized by the churches and shop-keepers of Lourdes, would have found in Fatima far less matter for indignation: all the features common to famous centres of pilgrimage are present—the devastated original site, the questionable buildings, the flood of pious gewgaws—but somehow their unpleasant effect is softened. Nevertheless, how much easier must it have been to offer up a prayer in the Cova da Iria of long ago!

We must now leave the high table-land, which has revealed an unexpected aspect of Portugal too often missing from the idyllic descriptions of the country, and resume our journey through the centres of art. Leiria, situated in a valley between the Liz and the Lena, is dominated by its medieval fortress built by Afonso I. This king built the keep, and often stayed at the castle with Queen Isabella. John I built the chapel of Nossa Senhora da Pena, in the Gothic style of Batalha, and the striking group of buildings is rounded off by the ruins of the palace. It is hard to decide which to admire more: the magician's castle nesting on the majestic acropolis of its lofty hill, or the view from the summit which stretches away to the spires of Batalha.

Batalha is our next destination. The intervening country reminds us,

From Tomar to Nazaré

in its mellow peace, of Périgord or the Loire valley. There are no marked features in this charming landscape—only a tender blue sky, gentle hills, and a mantle often frayed but never torn of flowers and green fields. On the doorsteps of their houses the peasants display their home-made pottery. The women wear black skirts with innumerable pleats, while their faces shine under the brilliant colours of their shawls.

On the left bank of the river Lena, in a rolling wooded valley, we cross a bridge and suddenly see below us the market town and the main façade of the monastery of Batalha. The façade and its doorway, in pale yellow stone with a shade of pink where the sun catches them, are in the peculiar Gothic style akin to, and probably influenced by, English Perpendicular. Yet these are but one feature of this monastery erected by many master-builders during many reigns, whose very name Batalha is a glorious reminder of the struggle for national independence. Before us rises a symphony of roofs and pinnacles and terraces, an endless proliferation of stone that dazzles the imagination.

In spite of this profusion of building and complicated history, the plan of the whole remains perfectly clear. The main doorway is on the west, with a side door on the south. There are two annexes: the Founder's chapel to the south-west, and at the east end the Unfinished Chapels. The nave, the chapter-house and the refectory lie parallel to the great or royal cloister which runs to the north of the church: King Afonso's cloister is still farther north.

Before the battle of Albujarrota in 1385 John I made a vow to build a monastery and dedicate it to the Virgin if he defeated the Spaniards, and the greater part of the buildings date from his reign (1388-1433). The work was entrusted to the Dominicans, and the first foreman was the Portuguese Afonso Domingues (1388-1402), who employed a national variant of Gothic combining a flavour of Romanesque with a tendency to simplification. In building the nave, the south door, the choir and the cloister and its outbuildings, the architect was inspired by the near-by monastery of Alcobaça and the cathedral at Evora. His successor, Ougete (1402-1438), was perhaps a bolder artist, and aided or influenced by English artists (Queen Philippa was a Lancastrian) employed a style nearer to the Gothic of York and Canterbury. He completed the church, put up the main façade (in the Perpendicular style) and its doorway, raised the roof of the great cloister and the even more daring roof of the chapter-house, built the Founder's chapel (that is, the chapel reserved for the tombs of the founder John I and his queen) and began the polygonal rotunda above the choir which King Duarte (1433–1438) proposed to make the Saint-Denis of his dynasty. Under the master-builders Martin Vasques and Fernão d'Evora (1438–1477) there is a reversion to a purely national style. Afonso V (1438–1481) added to this Dominican monastery an exquisite cloister, Gothic in style and Franciscan in spirit.

Up to that time each age and each architect had been content to contribute individual touches within the limits of a single style. Batalha, smiling or frowning in the sunshine, provided an example of Gothic in all its very human diversity. But now this forest of stone was overwhelmed in an irresistible flood of Manueline motifs, and the buildings exhibit a unique combination of poetry and strength. To Mateus Fernandes (1490–1515) we owe the monumental doorway of the Unfinished Chapels: Boytac was responsible for the screens in the royal cloister, that wonderful white marble lace-work which adorns the arches of the galleries. It was, however, the king who smothered the Unfinished Chapels with Manueline ornamentation. After his death they remained unfinished, to which circumstance they owe their name: John III, in fact, after having commissioned João de Castilho to build a loggia above the chapels, abandoned the project and devoted his energies to Belem and Tomar. And so for centuries the only roof they have known is the sky.

A lengthy visit is required to reveal the myriad beauties of these wonderful buildings. In contrast with the somewhat archaic geometrical motifs of the side doorway, the main door is crowded with sculpture: angels, saints, martyrs, popes and kings on the arching, Christ and the Evangelists on the tympanum, and the twelve Apostles (modern copies of the original statues) on the splays. The façade, in spite of the soaring effect produced by its perpendicular lines and innumerable pinnacles, suffers from being sited slightly below the level of the square in front of the church. All the more striking is the impression made by the interior, where the tall, spare and powerful nave runs straight through a cloud of warm golden colours, like a triumphal avenue for its victorious God. At the end of the nave, the dazzling Manueline stained-glass windows of the choir represent *The Visitation, The Adoration of the Magi, The Flight into Egypt* and *The Resurrection*. The Founder's chapel, with its ogives and foils and lacework, rears above our heads the perfect calyx of its starry dome. In the centre, at the head of a company of buried kings, John I and Queen Philippa lie hand in hand beneath two wonderful canopies. Along the walls are ranged the tombs of their sons the Infantes, the pride of Portugal: St Ferdinand, John the Grand Master of Santiago, Henry the Navigator and the Regent Peter, Duke of Coimbra; these few names and sepulchres evoke memories of the most glorious days of the dynasty of Aviz. To the west are the modern tombs of Afonso V, John II and his son Afonso.

We now enter the great cloister. However often and for however long one may have studied its wealth of architectural and decorative detail, its magical atmosphere never fails to charm: the simplicity of the arches, the Moorish delicacy of the screen-work, the Oriental appearance of the cool washing-fountain of the monks—and on every side a terrace looks out on the geometric blue patterns of roofs rising towards an even bluer sky. Under a gallery is the entrance to the chapter-house: the radiating nerves of the vault meet in the form of a star encircling a rosette, the Manueline stained-glass windows represent scenes from the Passion. No more impressive or moving setting could have been chosen for the resting-place of Portugal's two Unknown Soldiers who fell, one in Africa and the other fighting at our side in the First World War.

After the noble simplicity of the refectory, King Afonso's cloister exhales an intimate Franciscan charm: an Italian peace reigns beneath the pointed arches of the walled garden.

The last and greatest surprise awaits us in Batalha's Unfinished Chapels. Suddenly we come upon the grandiose portal erected for King Manuel by Mateus Fernandes, fronting the building already begun by King Duarte. A gushing fountain of stone breaks into a spray of lace, an inexhaustible intricacy of delicate ornamentation, a great arch joyfully displaying its sculptures to the steel-blue air. Each pillar soars gracefully upwards with no diminution of its vital force, the forest is never smothered under the proliferation of motifs. The portal is no mere entry to a collection of tombs, it is a triumphal arch opening on a heaven where kings lie at rest in the peace of God and the grateful memories of man. And as we enter, it is indeed the eternal light of heaven that shines on the tombs and on the surrounding chapels lying open to the air. Here rest King Duarte and Leonor of Aragon: the monarch, whose motto 'Leauté faray tà yaserey' was endlessly repeated by King Manuel in circles of ivy on the monumental portal, sleeps in enjoyment of the greatest gift his last palace could bestow, the immaculate sky of Batalha.

From a low hill a little way behind the monastery a view can be obtained of the whole range of buildings: a poem composed of pinnacles and roofs, of terraces and arcades, a symphony of soft stone frolicking in the hazy sunshine and the dust of the tree-tops. Our Lady of Victory, Batalha's unforgettable monastery, is a sight to ravish the mind and enthral the heart, whose memory no visitor to Portugal can recall without a pang.

At Belem, it is possible that a more stunning and unexpected effect is produced by the soaring vaults of the church, and the sculpture of the cloister certainly surpasses that of Batalha. The church and rooms of Alcobaça's Cistercian abbey are perhaps in a plainer, purer and statelier style. And there is Tomar on its high wooded hill in a delicate Tuscan setting, with its many cloisters clinging round the famous window like a colossal sheaf of flowers. But all these are forgotten under the vaults of Batalha's royal cloister, where one can no longer speak of stone-work or garden, still less of architecture and sculpture. Here all is peace and happiness, aristocratic elegance, a perfect harmony of light and roofs and church and endless flights of arcades: the great arches are like a religious cavalcade galloping into the luminous distance. Between the pillars the sun-drenched screens cast a leafy network on the shady walls. From its corner nook the fountain, scalloped like an altar cloth and cool as a chalice brimmed with snow, offers its waters to the thirsty doves. This royal cloister, under the square of sky framed by its four arcades, offers a foretaste of everlasting peace. The Unfinished Chapels keep their roofs open to the sky so that the still brightness of the sun and the serenity of the starry sky may shine unhindered on the sleeping dead. In these chapels whose triumphant arch is the gateway to the heavenly joys, the soul may for one brief moment taste a purity even greater than theirs.

On the way to Alcobaça we pass the actual site of the victory of 1385 to which Batalha owed its foundation. The chapel of St George at Albujarrota was built by the High Constable Nuño Alvares on the ground where he drew up his army, and Albujarrota itself is at the entrance to the valley where the battle was joined. The road traverses the heights bordering the valley, and looks over vast stretches of woodland in which a few villages form patches of darker green. The mountains in front of us are rugged, and scored by straight vertical channels worn by the falling streams. The landscape is bare and dry, in striking contrast with the poetic charm of the country round Batalha. But soon the woods and green fields are smiling once more, and the landscape stretches into the distance towards the sea, only a few miles beyond Alcobaça. A bend in the road suddenly discloses a wonderful picture of hills, tree-tops, flowers and the far-off Atlantic; a picture only to be gradually hidden again by the next twist of the road.

Alcobaça is a small town with lively markets for the sale of pottery and other articles of local product. In the centre of the town, looking on a vast square striped with numerous flower-beds, stands the façade of the monastery. As a result of alterations in the seventeenth and eighteenth centuries it has lost the true characteristics of an abbey, and conceals behind Baroque walls the Cistercian simplicity of the old monastery founded in 1152 on the fertile banks of the rivers Alcoa and Baça. The extent of the buildings bears witness to its former prosperity. They are a Portuguese reproduction of a type of Cistercian monastery like Clairvaux or Pontigny, running counter to the development of the national style with its favourite echoes of Romanesque. The naves of the church were made equal in height, in an attempt to improve the lighting; but as M. Elie Lambert has pointed out, their distinctive beauty derives from the upsurge of the vertical lines. The interior, impressive in its bareness, is of magnificent proportions, with an astonishing double line of dazzling columns stretching away towards the choir, beyond which a second perspective is provided by still more columns and by the vaults of the ambulatory and surrounding chapels. The whole effect, in its combination of purity and complexity, is like the threshold of Paradise.

The church contains many sculptures of the first importance. The life-size painted terra-cotta statues were made in the second half of the seventeenth century by the monks, one at least of whom is known to us by the name of Mestre Frei Pedro. In sincerity of religious feeling, combined in certain cases with charm or power, they represent one of the most interesting aspects of Portuguese art, particularly in a period subject to strong Spanish influence. Worth mentioning are a group, unfortunately mutilated, representing *The Death of St Bernard*, a lively and graceful angel with a musical instrument, and a noble Virgin of the Annunciation half awakened from her vision of the heavenly messenger.

The tombs of Inez de Castro and Pedro the Cruel combine formal beauty with the fascination of a tragic story. They are placed foot to foot in a chapel to the right of the transept, in order (so the tradition goes) that at the Resurrection the two risen lovers may meet again face to face. Both tombs were unfortunately damaged in 1811 by the troops of the Comte d'Erlon. Despite undeniable French influence, they are nevertheless authentic masterpieces of the Portuguese sculpture of the second half of the fourteenth century. From Portugal, as a matter of fact, come the superabundance of motifs such as the Moorish arch, found all over the peninsula, and perhaps also the iconography. But to Portugal, above all, belongs the story conjured up by the spectacle of these wonderful works of art: Inez supported by angels, the drama of the Last Judgment unfolding at her feet; and that enigmatic rosette on King Pedro's tomb in which some have seen the symbol of his love for Inez, while other more recent critics have interpreted it as Fortune's wheel. Everyone is familiar with the story of the 'dead queen' dramatized by H. de Montherlant, who, however, was less concerned to give a faithful rendering of the actors and personages of the drama than to focus attention on the character of Ferrante. It was impossible for Montherlant to deal with everything—the passionate love-affair, the hideous death, the horrible revenge—and it is to the legend itself that we must return, following its successive stages from lyric through tragedy to epic: the blissful hours by the banks of the Mondego, the murder at Santa Clara de Coimbra, Pedro's revenge after his accession to the throne, the torturing of his father's ministers, the royal honours paid to the unhappy woman's corpse. In these scenes of ruthless violence, close to the spirit if not to the historical truth of those passionate times, the Portugal of the Burgundian dynasty comes to life again, for legend is often a better interpreter than history of a nation's soul.

After the earthquake of 1755 nothing was left of King Manuel's sacristy but two doors, which show a combination of Renaissance and Manueline motifs. In the monks' cemetery, the eighteenth-century elegance of the little chapel of Our Lady of the Entombment contrasts with the noble severity of the principal outbuildings of the monastery, which date from the fourteenth century. Step by step we follow the monks in their daily tasks through these deserted rooms, still full of a Cistercian peace. The Cloister of Silence, which reminds one of Fontfroide, Poblet and Tarragona, was built between 1308 and 1311, an additional story being added in King Manuel's reign: the fourteenth-century lavabo has a Renaissance fountain. The enormous size of the dormitory and of the kitchen (through which a conduit runs from the river Alcoa) gives some idea of the importance of the monastery, whose abbot was one of the great personages of the realm. Perhaps the most beautiful and exciting of all the rooms is the refectory, where the arches of the reading loft under the plain roof seem designed to add a note of Italian cheerfulness to the solemn recital of the Office for the day.

Beyond Alcobaça we approach the sea. A line of sand-dunes cuts across the fields, and a totally different stretch of sand and pinewood brings us to Nazaré. The town consists of the *praia*, by the sea-shore, and the *sitio*, on top of the cliff more than a hundred metres above the beach. Nothing could surpass the beach at Nazaré for picturesque effect. On the sandy crescent lined by fishermen's houses the gaudy-coloured boats are drawn up ready to put to sea. A large area is covered with nets spread out to dry. The women, wearing felt hats and wrapped in long black shawls, squat gossiping and waiting for their men. Yokes of oxen stand by to haul the boats up the shore. As soon as the boats touch land, men, women and children lend a hand with the ropes, urging on the oxen to the accompaniment of a steady rhythmic chant, the only sound to be heard in the immensity of the silent *praia*. One is reminded perhaps of Phoenicia, or of the noble simplicity of a scene from the Bible.

The streets are thronged with fishermen dressed in plaids, their faces tanned by wind, sun and sea, their eyes strangely bright. The women have discarded their black shawls, and their hips sway under several thicknesses of coloured skirts. This, we recognize, is the genuine Portugal—and the people of Nazaré do not in the least mind being stared at: it is they who are the *grands seigneurs*, not the foreigners who gape at them with brazen curiosity.

As seen from the *sitio* the spectacle is even finer. All along the beach the pattern of nets and tiny boats and the black blobs of the fishermen is spread out like a draughtboard. The boats crawl slowly up the beach, drawn by their teams of oxen. Nazaré, a motley, peaceful hive of industry, breathes like a righteous people safe in the hand of God. And indeed it was at Nazaré, in 1182, that a certain Fuas Roupinho, when out stag-hunting, would have been precipitated into the sea, had not the Virgin miraculously intervened and pulled up his horse, an event commemorated by the pilgrimage shrine of Nossa Senhora de Nazaré.

A few miles farther south is the beach of San Martinho de Porto, set in its ring-shaped cove. There are many places to be visited before we reach our destination in Lisbon. Near the island of Berlenga is the little port of Peniche, joined to the mainland by a tongue of land bounded by tall cliffs, with attractive views out to sea. Inland is the spa, dating from Queen Leonor's time, of Caldas da Rainha, a town celebrated not only for its mineral springs but for the pottery of R. Bordalo Pinheiro. The church of Nossa Senhora do Pópulo has a Manueline belfry, and contains a triptych attributed to Cristovão de Figueiredo. Finally there is the castle of Obidos, an impressive assembly of buildings consisting of fortifications, keep and baronial hall. This medieval vision of lofty walls and regular battlements forms a worthy end to a journey as rich in history and art as could be found in any country within so restricted a space.

        61. EN BEIRA
          IN BEIRA
        62. TOMAR
          LE COUVENT DU CHRIST
          THE MONASTERY OF CHRIST

63 à 66. TOMAR.
COUVENT DU CHRIST. DÉTAILS.
THE MONASTERY OF CHRIST. DETAILS.

ROTONDE DE
L'ÉGLISE DES
TEMPLIERS.

ROTUNDA OF
THE CHURCH
OF THE
TEMPLARS.

TOMAR.
COUVENT
DU CHRIST.

THE MONASTERY
OF CHRIST.

SAINT JÉRÔME.
ST. JEROME.

68

69

70

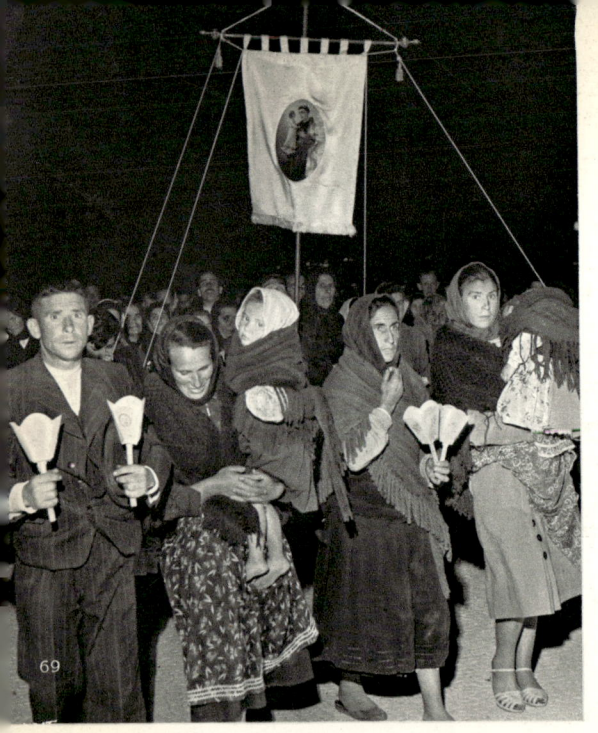

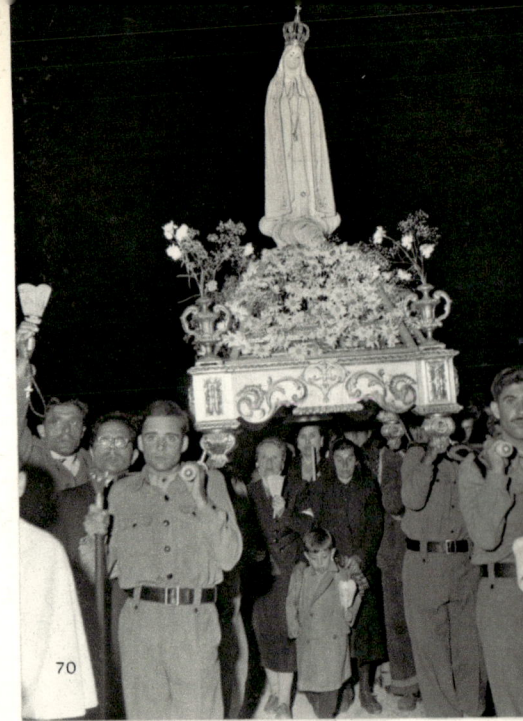

69 à 72.
PÈLERINAGE À NOTRE-DAME DE FATIMA.
PILGRIMS AT FATIMA.

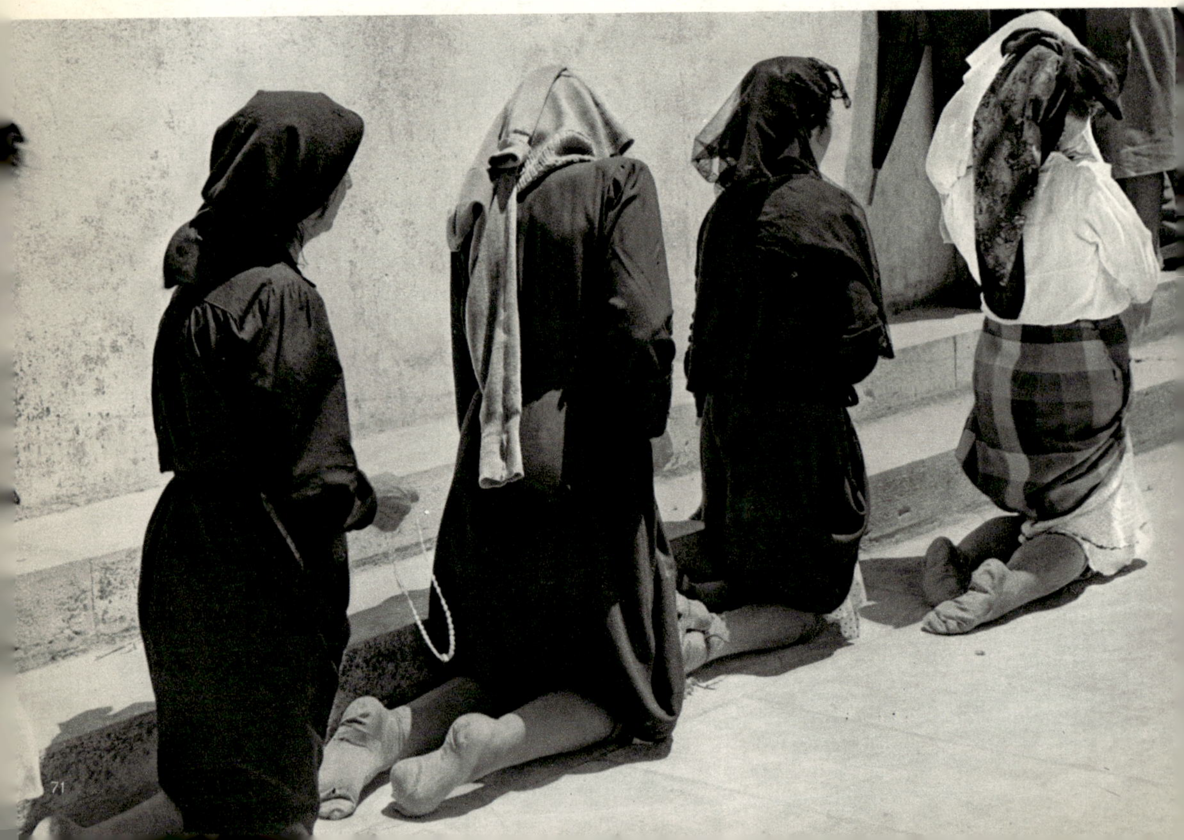

71

73. LEIRIA VU DU CHÂTEAU.
    LEIRIA SEEN FROM THE CASTLE

74. MONASTÈRE DE BATALHA. LES CHAPELLES IMPARFAIT
    THE BATALHA MONASTERY. THE UNFINISHED CHAPEL

75.
MONASTÈRE DE BATALHA.
THE BATALHA MONASTERY.

76-77.
MONASTÈRE DE BATALHA.
LE CLOÎTRE ROYAL.
THE BATALHA MONASTERY.
ROYAL CLOISTER.

78-79. BATALHA.
LES CHAPELLES IMPARFAITES.
PORTAIL ET VOÛTE DE MATEUS FERNANDES.
THE UNFINISHED CHAPELS.
PORTAL AND VAULTING OF MATEUS FERNANDES.

80. ALCOBAÇA.
MONASTÈRE SANTA MARIA.
TOMBEAU DE DOM PEDRO. DÉTAIL.
THE SANTA MARIA MONASTERY.
DETAIL OF DOM PEDRO'S TOMB.

81. ALCOBAÇA.
MONASTÈRE
SANTA MARIA.
MAUSOLÉE D'INÈS DE
CASTRO ET DE DOM
PEDRO I.
THE SANTA MARIA
MONASTERY.
MAUSOLEUM OF INES
DE CASTRO AND
DOM PEDRO I.

82. ALCOBAÇA.
MONASTÈRE SANTA MARIA. LE RÉFECTOIRE DES MOINES.
THE SANTA MARIA MONASTERY. THE MONKS' REFECTORY.

83 à 93. PÊCHEURS ET FEMMES DE NAZARÉ.
FISHERS AND WOMEN OF NAZARÉ.

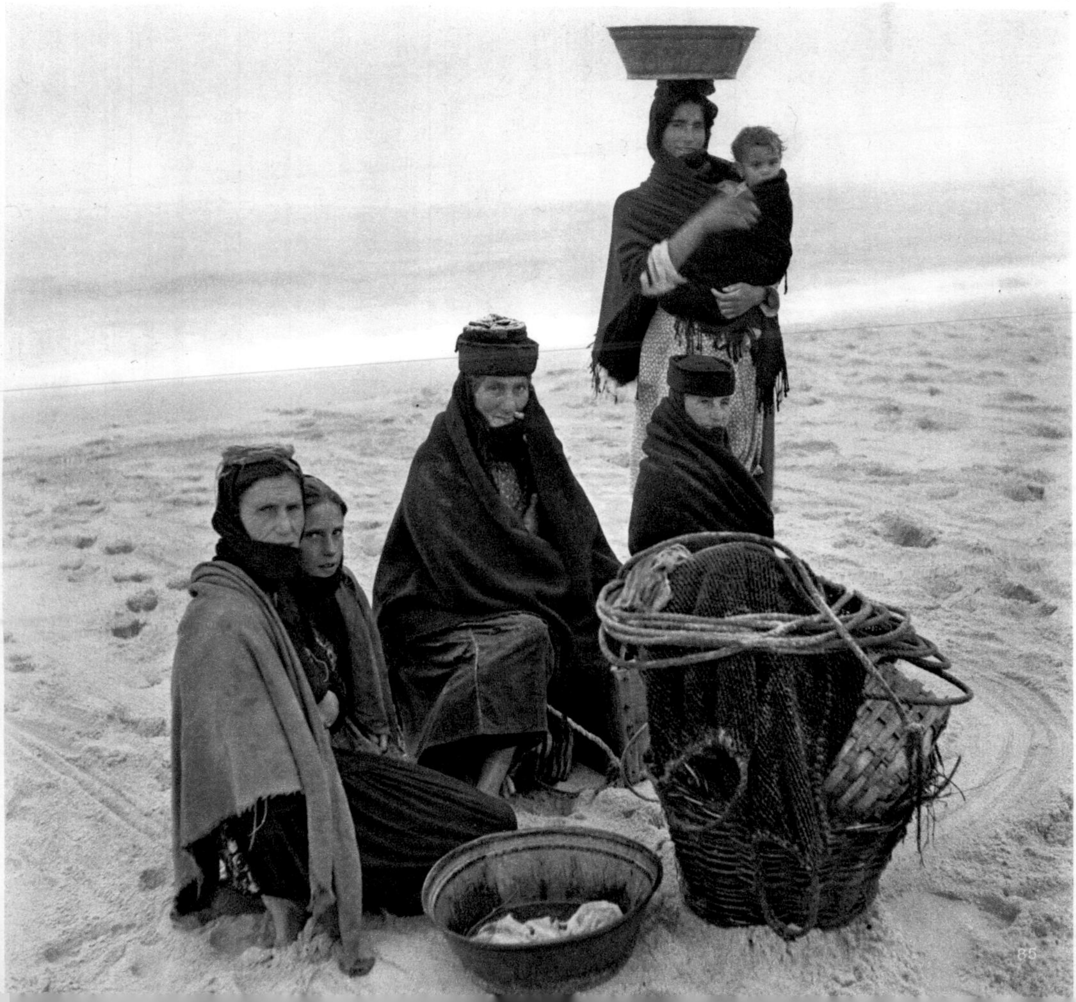

CHAPTER IV

Lisbon and the Banks of the Tagus

LISBON, the city of the Atlantic and the Tagus, is best approached not by road but by river. Near the capital, the river opens out into the Sea of Straw—a poetic but not always appropriate name, since its waters are sometimes leaden in colour, though more often, in the capricious light of this oceanic climate, they sparkle with a thousand golden straws, like a cargo of hay left sole survivor of a catastrophic shipwreck. The city's unique quality reveals itself on the stretch between the Lisbon docks and Barreiro and Cacilhas to the south. Lisbon is a port covering many miles in length, and the sea, from which for centuries she has derived wealth and fame, is her life-blood. With her 800,000 inhabitants she is perhaps too swollen a capital for a country the size of Portugal.

If we sail slowly down the misty river, threading a way through the small boats bending their grateful sails to the perfumed breeze, we notice that on the north, industrial bank the sky is obscured by the smoke from the factories; whereas the low, unbuilt-on south bank is mysteriously sheltered by green fields and trees. If, on the other hand, we sail up the few miles of estuary between the ocean and the Sea of Straw, we shall salute on our way Cascais and Estoril, and then the tower of Belem, which once stood in mid-stream but has since shifted by silting to the south bank. Or we can approach from Cacilhas, gradually picking out the principal features and buildings of Lisbon. The docks stretch away into the distance; the steamers alongside screen the city; a far-off sailing-boat suddenly blots out part of the sky. We marvel at the houses piled up on the hills (Lisbon, like Rome, is built on seven hills), at the sea of buildings and roofs intersected by strips of greenery, at the apparition of belfries and church towers. One by one the principal monuments come into sight. To the right, the battlemented castle of St George towers over the city which for so long it defended. In the centre of the smoky line of docks we can make out a rectangular opening—the Praça do Comercio, generally known as the Terreiro do Paço, lined on three sides by uniform buildings and open on the fourth side to the Tagus, into which it plunges by a marble landing-stage adorned with two columns—the *pais das colunas*. Mounting the steps, we find ourselves at once in the square at the heart of the city as it was rebuilt by the Marquès de Pombal after the earthquake of 1755.

This fateful date and this statesman's name crop up continuously during a visit to the present capital of Portugal. The catastrophe was so great and the genius of Pombal so brilliant that the city's past seems almost buried in oblivion. Yet in fact Lisbon has had a long and glorious history. By the Romans it was called Felicitas Julia in honour of Julius Caesar. The Visigoths surrounded it with ramparts, and for a long time it was occupied by the Moors, who were expelled by King Afonso I with the help of Crusaders on their way to the East. Afonso III made it his capital and royal seat. The university has been several times moved backwards and forwards between Coimbra and Lisbon. At the beginning of the sixteenth century, thanks to Portugal's overseas discoveries, Lisbon attained its height of wealth and fame: the city became one of the most prosperous, and its port one of the busiest, in the western hemisphere. The loss of its independence reduced it to the second rank as the seat of a viceroy. On the restoration of the monarchy by the house of Braganza, the capital enjoyed a second period of great prosperity in the reign of the extravagant John V. Then, on 1st November 1755, an earthquake, whose shock was felt all over the Iberian peninsula, destroyed the city, causing irreparable damage, including the loss of a vast quantity of treasure from the Indies, and tens of thousands of deaths. The shocks were followed by a terrible fire which completed the work of destruction. The worst of the damage was done on the banks of the Tagus, on the site of the present Baixa, or lower town. Portugal's only good fortune was to have the Marquès de Pombal at the head of affairs. It was he who instructed two engineers, Eugénio dos Santos and Manuel da Maia, to build the new city to a regular plan. Beyond the noble Praça do Comercio there sprang up a veritable chequer-work of streets, intersecting at right angles and producing, it must be confessed, a somewhat monotonous effect. The visitor who, relying on travellers' tales, expects to find a kind of Place de la Concorde backed by an eighteenth-century French town, is likely to be disappointed with the reality. The Terreiro do Paço, on the site of the pre-1755 Paço da Ribeira, is an incomparable harmony of line—arcades and tall towers—and colour—a green touched off by the light—and looks out over the wonderful scenery of the Sea of Straw; but it bears only a superficial resemblance to the Place de la Concorde. It is true that the original conception of both was the same: both are 'royal squares' designed as a setting for the statue of the monarch: Bouchardon's *Louis XV* in Paris and Machado de Castro's *Joseph I* in Lisbon. But Gabriel's buildings carry on the architectural tradition of the Louvre colonnade, whereas the Praça do Comercio buildings have a touch of the operatic in their undeniable stateliness. The Place de la Concorde is actually an urban landscape, whereas the Praça is open to the Tagus and impregnated with the smell of the sea. Moreover, the Terreiro do Paço is a far more successful specimen of architecture than the geometrically designed quarter immediately to its north: its principal merit is its regularity. Yet how quickly one tires of those identical façades and streets all the same, of those grey perspectives receding into the distance, under the cables of the electric trams suspended above the noisy crowded streets!

Let us pause for a while under the arcades of the square, where a royal welcome always awaits even the humblest visitor. The buildings surrounding us are government offices: at the corner of the Rua de l'Arsenal is the General Post Office, near the scene of the assassination on 1st February 1908 of King Carlos and the Crown Prince, a double crime which two years later was to lead to the downfall of the monarchy, and whose tragic memory still haunts the bustling square. Close at hand, by the river, are the South, the South East and the Cais do Sodré railways stations. The Terreiro do Paço is the unavoidable way through to the old quarters in Belem to the east, and from Belem to Estoril and Cascais. It is always thronged with cars and trams and pedestrians—but the Tagus, too, is always close at hand to offer its boundless view.

The streets of the Baixa lead from the square to the noisy commercial centre of the city: they are the Rua da Prata (the Street of Silver), the Rua do Ouro (the Street of Gold) and the Rua Augusta which runs through the great central arch. The Praça de D. Pedro IV, generally known as the Rossio and flanked on one side by the Maria II Theatre, together with the Praça dos Restauradores near the Central Station, constitute the liveliest district in Lisbon, where the revolving batons of the impassive police do their best to direct the crowds of pedestrians and the streams of German and American cars: a deafening clamour rises from the innumerable shops and cafés and swarms of people talking and shouting and drinking. The Praça dos Restauradores is dedicated to the heroes who rose against Spain on 1st December 1640, and thus brought about the restoration of Portuguese independence: their valour is commemorated by an obelisk. On the same square stands one of the loveliest buildings in Lisbon, the Palacio Foz, now the offices of the National Secretariats of Information and of Tourism. Above, on a gentle slope lined with modern buildings, runs the long Avenida da Liberdade, which in liveliness and architectural style reminds one of the Champs-Élysées, while its green lawns recall the Castellana in Madrid. At the top, where the streets meet and intersect, is the Praça Marquês de Pombal, in which the titles and achievements of the great statesman are commemorated by a tall statue and by inscriptions let into the ground: from the square there is a fine view over the city in the direction of the Tagus. Still higher up, our way passes through the Edward VII Park. On reaching the *estufa fria* (a cool-house, one of the sights of Lisbon, full of flourishing tropical plants) we can turn and enjoy the view of Lisbon, with its sea of greenery and grey stones rivalling the waters of the Tagus.

Farther to the north-east we reach the most modern quarters. The church of Nossa Senhora da Fatima, built by Pardal Monteiro and containing statues of the Apostles by Francisco Franco, is a fine example of contemporary Portuguese art. The Praça de Touros reminds us of the popularity of bull-fighting in Portugal, in spite of the fact that since Pombal's time the kill has been banned. A great deal of admirable new building has been carried out by the Salazar government and, in particular, the Minister Duarte Pacheco: the vast new quarters with their charming houses have lost nothing of the traditional felicity of style, the most attractive perhaps being the Alameda de D. Henriques with its fountains and gaily painted houses. Beyond this avenue is the way out from Lisbon to the airport and the road along the river to Vila Franca de Xira. The interminable, straight Rua Almirante Reiss brings us back to the Rossio Square.

The section of Lisbon through which we have just passed may be briefly compared to a fan, spread out above its handle resting on the Praça do Comercio. Between it and the Tagus there are two vast districts waiting to be explored: the east quarters, the oldest and most picturesque; and the west, the most interesting from the artistic point of view.

East Lisbon is dominated by the castle of St George, a medieval fortress which was also a royal seat. It is worth making the steep climb up to the old walls to enjoy the incomparable view of the city and the river. The space inside the outer wall, once dedicated to warlike purposes, is now occupied by peaceful gardens and terraces, where the young soldiers, like their fellows all over the world, flirt with the nursemaids while they keep an eye on their unruly charges. Picturesque narrow streets lead to the church of Craça, rebuilt at the end of the last century and containing in the sacristy the tomb of Afonso de Albuquerque. Near the church is held the *feira da ladra*, a flea market where every conceivable kind of bric-à-brac is for sale—including perhaps a dubious masterpiece or two. A view as fascinating as that from the castle can be enjoyed from the belvedere of Nossa Senhora do Monte, in which there is a chapel dedicated to St Gens, the first bishop of Lisbon. The church of São Vicente de Fora, rebuilt by Filippo Terzi, is one of the most interesting in the capital: it is built of limestone looking like marble, in a design modelled on that of the Gesù in Rome. The cloister has a wonderful collection of *azulejos* picturing the Fables of La Fontaine, while in the old monastic buildings there are more *azulejos* representing the capture of Lisbon and Santarem. The church is, above all, famous for its royal Pantheon containing the coffins of the Braganza kings and queens, among others those of King Carlos and Queen Amelia. Close by is the round church of Santa Engracia, containing some magnificent marbles, begun in 1682 and not yet completed.

Lisbon and the Banks of the Tagus

Close to the docks and the river is the Arsenal do Exercito, now the Military Museum. The rooms, which are decorated with *boiseries* and some of whose ceilings are by Columbano, contain a collection of armour and pictures. The convent of Madre de Deus was founded by Leonor, widow of John II, added to by John III and rebuilt after the earthquake. Situated in an industrial quarter little frequented by tourists, it is well worth a visit for the sake of its artistic treasures. Over the Manueline door can be seen the fillet and the pelican, emblems of Leonor and John II. In the nave we breath once more the enchanted air of the gilt woodwork found in so many eighteenth-century churches: a mysterious everlasting springtime seems to blossom in the leaf-work covering the walls. In striking contrast with this riot of decoration is the formal serenity of the adjacent Renaissance cloister. Even lovelier is another tiny cloister built shortly after the convent was founded: its Manueline arcade frames a well against the sky, and the foot falls as lightly on the earth as the splash of a pebble in the water; the whole atmosphere breathes a gentle feminine charm.

The Romanesque cathedral, or Sé, whose massive outline can be easily distinguished below the castle, is probably the work of the masters Robert and Bernard who built the old cathedral of Coimbra, and may be dated half-way between the latter (1160) and the cathedral of Evora (1186–1283). The cloister dates from about 1332, and is modelled on that of Alcobaça. The church was rebuilt after the earthquakes of 1344 and 1755. The glorious history of Lisbon lives again under the noble simplicity of the vaults and in the many sculptures of exceptional beauty: in the choir, the tombs of Afonso IV and Beatrix by Machado de Castro are replacements of the originals destroyed in 1755. By the same artist there is a Crib crowded with figures, whose delicate execution and earthy savour combine to produce a perfect example of its familiar kind. . . . Near the cathedral is the church of Santo Antonio de Sé, rebuilt at the end of the eighteenth century on the spot where St Anthony of Padua was born.

It is now time to return to the Praça do Comercio and plunge into Lisbon's most picturesque quarter, the Alfama; a network of narrow precipitous streets where the fisherfolk live. The stones exude a smell of fish and antiquity; overhead the washing is hung out to dry, and above it the glorious sun throws a sudden beam on the leprous walls; children surge up from every nook and corner, deaf to their mothers' call; and the mothers' shrill cries are answered by the headlong rush of their offspring down the flights of steps. There are moments when we seem to see, buried beneath Pombal's Lisbon, the original city and its ancient seafaring folk. There is an air of popular poetry about this district, with its gable windows and barred windows, its overhanging stories, and its earthenware Virgins and saints. Sometimes we come to a dead-end, as in São Miguel or Bicha Alley, and are forced to retrace our steps. . . . But we must extricate ourselves from this fascinating maze, and proceed under the archway of the Travessa de São João de Parça till we reach the Casa dos Bicos, so called from the pointed cut stones composing its façade, like the house of the same name in Segovia. A few yards farther on, we come upon a remarkable Manueline façade with a fine door flanked by two windows: this is the remains of the church of Conceição Velha which was built by King Manuel and rebuilt after the earthquake of 1755: on the tympanum there are sculptures of the King, Queen Leonor, Pope Leo X and various other personages.

Every lover of the picturesque will carry away precious memories from the eastern quarters of Lisbon: the western quarters, on the other hand, will make a special appeal to the lover of art.

Right in the centre of the city, but overlooking it with its terraces, we find a first belt of buildings and museums and interesting sights. Before the earthquake the Carmo Convent was 'the most important Gothic building in Lisbon'. It was built on the same plan as the monastery of Batalha by Nuño Alvares Pereira, the victor of Albujarrota (1393–1423). The silent ruins and roofless bays now house an archaeological museum containing several fine sarcophagi: Ferdinand I (fourteenth century), Gonçalo de Sousa (fifteenth century) and Rui de Meneses (1528). The Rua Garrett (or the Chiado, to give it its local nickname) is Lisbon's Bond Street, and runs close by the San Carlos Theatre and the Praça de Camões, where there is a monument of the poet surrounded by eight

Portuguese chroniclers commemorating (not very happily) the famous author of *The Lusiads*. In the neighbouring quarter there are well-known night clubs where you can listen to the *fado*, that traditional song whose rasping melancholy seems to be yearning for an infinitely remote past. The audience takes up the words of the song, and even the most insular and impervious foreigner cannot resist the seductive sadness of even a simple love song. Among the museums (with which Lisbon is plentifully supplied) we can admire the beautiful collection of plate in the Museum of Sacred Art and the Columbano paintings in the Museum of Modern Art. And now let us enter the church of São Roque, built by Filippo Terzi at the end of the sixteenth century. Behind the façade, restored after the earthquake, is the magnificent chapel built by John V and dedicated to St John the Baptist. This fine example of mid-eighteenth-century art in Lisbon was designed by Salvi and Vanvitelli, with mosaics by Maretti and Masucci of agate, lapis lazuli, amethyst, ivory, bronze and marble. Continuing through the Botanical Gardens, which has a collection of exotic trees, we reach the Estrêla, modelled on St Peter's at Rome, containing the tomb of Queen Maria I and, in the sacristy, that of her confessor, probably the work of Machado de Castro.

A steep descent now brings us back to the docks district, and to the Rua das Janelas Verdes, in which the Museum of Ancient Art contains some of the finest works of art in the capital.

The museum is housed in the former palace of the counts of Alvor and Pombal, which has been enlarged and adapted, on the site of the Carmelite convent of Santo Alberto, of which only the chapel remains. The position itself of the museum, looking out as it does on a narrow old street, the busy docks and a small square planted with flowers, is characteristic of Lisbon in its combination of ancient city, great port and ubiquitous gardens. Its attraction is due not only to the variety and comprehensiveness of the exhibits, but to the taste with which they are displayed, so that the visitor might fancy himself a privileged guest in the private house of some wealthy collector. There is a very complete collection of Portuguese painting, the chief European schools (except the French and English) being also well represented, a section devoted to sculpture, pottery and religious art, and a wonderful collection of plate containing objects not only of intrinsic beauty but of unique historical interest. Here, for instance, is the silver Romanesque chalice from the monastery of Alcobaça, and the cross of Sancho I from the Santa Cruz Monastery at Coimbra; and here is the custodial, made of gold from the Indies, which Manuel I had wrought by the poet-goldsmith Gil Vicente for the monastery of Belem in 1506: the Apostles are represented grouped round the niche containing the Host. One whole room is devoted to French eighteenth-century plate, probably a unique collection in view of the disappearance of the French royal plate. It is true that the Germain brothers exaggerated their Baroque style to please the Braganza kings, but the beauty of their creations remains indisputable: for example, the statuettes by Cousinet representing couples of various nationalities have an elaborate gracefulness and a capricious charm very characteristic of their period.

The main attraction is naturally provided by the paintings. Quillard's *Fête dans un Parc* not only shows the influence of Watteau, but proves what an important part his pupil played in eighteenth-century Portugal, where Pillement also enjoyed great popularity. And there are many other enchanting pictures. An *Apostolado* by Zurbaran recalls the many masterpieces by this artist in the Spanish galleries at Guadaloupe, Seville, Cadiz or Madrid. A *Temptation of St Anthony* by J. Bosch is one of this master's most disquieting pictures, a fantastic world infested by terrifying demons and abandoned by the grace of God. With this we may contrast Gérard David's *Repos dans la Fuite en Egypte*, in which the Virgin peacefully suckles her Child, with the ass browsing at her side. Another Flemish Virgin, by Hans Memling, radiates the joy of the divine motherhood; and a painting by Mabuse shows a town with tall towers set in a smiling landscape, with the Virgin surrounded by angels with outspread wings. The museum also contains most of the fragments of the retable *The Sorrows of the Virgin* painted by Quentin Metsys about 1500 for the Madre de Deus Church, including the touching figure of the sorrowful Mother, her heart transfixed with grief. Dürer's *Saint Jerome* depicts the saint with a long curling beard, his finger resting on a skull, like a Renaissance thinker intent on plumbing the mysteries of science

Lisbon and the Banks of the Tagus

and penetrating the enigma of human life—an aged Erasmus rather than St Jerome in the desert. In a picture by Lucas Cranach we see the gaunt, vicious face of Salome, wearing beneath her head-dress of fur an inscrutable expression of indifference to the evil she has caused, and displaying to future ages the boon obtained from her indulgent father, the Baptist's head.

These pictures, beautiful as they are, can be matched in other of the world's galleries: what cannot be studied anywhere else is the evolution of the Portuguese school. There are pictures by Sequeira of his daughter, with a delicate almost sickly face, and of a foppish Conde de Farrobo whose elegant vanity and pretty little face, humorous but empty, recalls Goya's portrait of his own son. Domingos Vieira's portrait of Isabella de Moura shows the astonishing head of a woman draped in a snow-white cloak and hood. The expression of the face is arresting in its intensity, and even the lace, trailing like ivy, seems to stir with a mysterious vegetable life. Another striking picture, not unlike certain portraits by Philippe de Champaigne, represents an old nun telling her beads, dressed in a black habit and white veil, with the thin lips and hard eyes of advancing years. Frei Carlos brings to Portuguese painting a breath of Flemish sweetness and tender spirituality; his gentle mysticism is seen in *The Good Shepherd* and *Christ's Appearance to the Virgin*. Many works by unknown artists, such as the Master of the *Retable of the life of St James* and the Master of the *Retable of Santa Auta*, display religious feeling, attention to picturesque detail and originality of landscape, the figures in their pictures being purely Portuguese in type. The portrait by Cristovão de Morais of King Sebastian in splendid armour shows the young man already dreaming of the dramatic Alcacer-Kebir expedition which was to lead indirectly to the loss of national independence. Lastly, before we come to the museum's acknowledged masterpiece, there is an *Ecce Homo* in which the crucified Christ hides His ravaged face from the world He has redeemed.

In this necessarily hasty survey of Portuguese painting, in which we could give only a cursory attention to so many objects of interest and delight, we have gone backwards in time, leaving to the last the greatest masterpiece of all—the polyptych by Nuno Gonçalves of *The Veneration of St Vincent*. The six panels no doubt originally enclosed a statue of the saint, the two larger panels folding back on the smaller. Thus King Afonso V and his court, the Crown Prince (later King John II), the Infante Henry the Navigator, the Queen and possibly Gonçalves himself faced the Archbishop and his clergy, while the four side-panels pictured the dukes of Braganza, the presentation of St Vincent's relic, the fishermen and the monks of Alcobaça.

No words can adequately describe this *Veneration*: simply to gaze at it provides a perpetual feast to the eye. It is a miracle of damasked greens and dark reds, of flax-white and crimson, of leather, armour, silk and gold; a blaze of colour in which there is nothing exaggerated or superfluous. It is a high relief, a gathering of giants in a setting which is not of this world. We shrink to nothing before its overwhelming impact, and no other picture can live beside it. Every individual figure composing it is rendered with magical skill: the youthful saintly deacon, solemn and handsome, overflowing with divine love, bearing himself nobly like a page at the Court of Heaven; the manly princes in their finery; the knights stiffened in prayer, rightly seduced by this Veneration from their business of war or exploration; the fisherman with his net, bearing himself as proudly as the king, and his daringly foreshortened companion kneeling in prayer; the monks in their white flowing gowns.

According to the brilliant description of M. R. Huyghe, this polyptych was the first triumph of 'individualism': in it, for the first time in the western world, we hear 'the song of man's solitude'. In these six panels, huge and proud as a monumental frieze, each person, though a participant in the same ceremony, appears as if walled up in his own incommunicable personality, blind to the presence of his fellows. From one point of view the general effect is that of a group of solitaries, of 'strangers'. But this innovating quality of the painting should not be allowed to blind us to another of its aspects. *The Veneration of St Vincent* is not only a religious but a social performance: not only its subject, but also the very fact that it was painted at all, prove the vitality of fifteenth-century society in Portugal. On the one hand the juxtaposition of different social classes is a testimony to the unity of the country; on the other hand a quite different spirit is conveyed by the placing of these individualized people in a setting which still belongs formally to the Middle Ages. It is an apparently paradoxical situation, foreseen by the painter and vindicated by the history of the great discoveries of later times.

Of this society no more beautiful evocation can be imagined than the painting of Nuno Gonçalves. Thanks to him the golden age of the Aviz dynasty lives for ever: the glorious reign of John II, the voyages of discovery instigated by Henry the Navigator, the spiritual reputation of the monks, the picturesque nobility of the fisherfolk.... Gonçalves is an artist of startling originality, and in his monumental conception unique; not only does he dispense with the landscape so popular with the Flemish school, but he endows his painting with a concentration not to be found in van Eyck's *Adoration of the Lamb*, the work with which our polyptych immediately challenges comparison. Like *Las Meninas* and a very few other paintings, *The Veneration of St Vincent* is not a reproduction of life, it is life itself.

We must now continue our journey to Restelo, now called Belem. On the way we pass the Necessidades Palace, set in the midst of gardens, built for John V: it was a royal residence until the fall of the monarchy, and is now the Ministry of Foreign Affairs. Close by on the hillside is the vast Ajuda Park leading to the Ajuda Palace, which was begun at the beginning of the nineteenth century and remains unfinished. At the foot of the hill, on the Praça Afonso de Albuquerque, stands the Palace of Belem, the residence of the President of the Republic: its former riding-school houses the Coach Museum, one of the most important of its kind in Europe. All the pomp of the court of Braganza is revealed in the gilding and paintings on these royal coaches built in the seventeenth and eighteenth centuries in Portugal, Italy, Spain or France. Particularly elegant is John V's coach, sculpted by José and Felix Vicente de Almeida. The most gorgeous, if not the most beautiful, is the state coach built for the Marquês de Fontes, ambassador of the renowned John V at the court of Pope Clement XI (1716), with magnificent gilt-wood allegorical groups, particularly on the body-work, celebrating the nautical exploits of the country and the patronage extended by the king to art and letters.

We are now only a few yards from the Hieronymite monastery of Belem, whose proportions have unfortunately been spoilt by the addition of a long, nineteenth-century Manueline building, now the home of the Vasconcelos Ethnological Museum. In spite of this, the monastery remains the most beautiful building in Lisbon, and is with Batalha, Alcobaça and Tomar one of the most unforgettable treasures of Portuguese art.

The monastery was founded in 1497 by King Manuel out of the wealth provided by the voyages of discovery, and stands on the site of a chapel founded by Henry the Navigator. Work was begun in 1502 and continued until 1516 under the direction of Boytac, to whom we owe the design of the church and cloister and, in general, the Manueline features of the various buildings. After his departure, probably to Batalha, João de Castilho, employing a very different style, completed the south door of the church, the vault and columns of the nave, the sacristy, and the cloister with the exception of the Renaissance columns and arches. Work on the west door (1517) was directed by Nicolas Chanterène, after which Diogo de Torralva took over, while Jean de Rouen completed the *capela-mor*.

In contemplating this wonderful building one cannot help regretting that it should have been stranded so far inland! In spite of the sun-kissed stone and sculptures of the monastery, the Tagus seems miles away, separated from us by the boulevards, the Cascais railway and the docks. One would have liked this building, endowed with the riches brought from across the seas, to be freshened by the waters of the river and sweetened by its breezes laden with so many glorious memories. Boytac's south door contrasts with Chanterène's, which reminds us of Champmol and looks ahead to the Santa Cruz at Coimbra. Among other statues the master-sculptor Nicolas was responsible for the kneeling figures of King Manuel and Queen Maria attended by their patron saints. The aery nave, which seems to float on its slender fantastically decorated columns, and the even lighter transept with its columns like celestial reeds are far more attractive than the rather heavy *capela-mor*, which has a retable of the Passion attributed to Cristovão Lopes. In the church are the royal tombs of King Manuel and Queen Maria, John III and Catherine of Austria and their children, King Sebastian and the Cardinal King Henry. Camoëns and Vasco da Gama are also buried here in neo-Manueline tombs. The roof of the sacristy is supported by the spreading stone branches of a single central column smothered with Renaissance decoration.

Near the chapter-house, where Marshal Carmona lies buried, we pass into the fairyland of the cloister, a wonderfully proportioned composition of stone arches sprouting with Manueline or Renaissance decorative motifs. The mind is troubled and overwhelmed by the exquisite happiness radiating from this masterpiece even more than by its superb proportions. In the cloister of Belem there reigns an unfamiliar peace, a tranquil Oriental bliss. The building's original purpose—to serve as an ambulatory for the monks and a vestibule to the church and its outbuildings—is here overstepped. At Alcobaça and Batalha the air we breathed was a Christian, monastic air. Under the trappings of art the imagination could still perceive the utilitarian function of the arcades, and picture the monks of old pacing beneath them. But at Belem these practical uses are only a pretext to transport us to some paradise from the *Arabian Nights*. This cloister is unlike all others in owing almost nothing to ecclesiastical art: it is a purely artistic flight of fancy rather than an embodiment of monastic peace.

The Museum of Popular Art, founded in 1940 and occupying a brand new building of exquisite proportions, contains exhibits illustrating the folklore of every province in Portugal—festivals, markets and pilgrimages. This dazzling display of enchanting costumes, everyday objects and unfamiliar customs is offered for the convenience of the traveller pressed for time, unfortunately unable to appreciate for himself the spirit of this land of peasants and mariners.

A Moorish note is struck by the tower of Belem, built by Francisco de Arruda, the brother of Diogo, whom he accompanied on his voyage to Morocco. In its proportions, however, the tower retains a certain Romanesque solidity and Gothic grace. A smell of seaweed and a whiff from the tide permeate the rooms beneath their perfect vaulting. If we mount to the top, with our heads still full of the Gonçalves polyptych, the spell of Belem and the treasures of the museum, the very site of this tower will open our eyes to what Lisbon really is: a city on the watch for the riches and discoveries lying in wait across the sea.

The time has now come to explore the environs of Lisbon, which are served by an excellent system of motorways. Just within the city boundary we can take a look at the Montes Claros promontory and the recently constructed stadium, built in tiers on the slopes of a hill and open on one side to the river; and in Benfica we can admire the rooms and gardens of the Casa dos Marquêses da Fronteira.

To the west of Lisbon runs a succession of beaches and rocky sites extending along the estuary to the sea-shore, the two best known and the most attractive being Estoril and Cascais. Estoril owes its charm to its gardens and wooded hills dotted with luxurious villas: here many European royalties have come to spend their days of exile. The shabby beach is unworthy of the famous spa and watering-place. Cascais is a picturesque little port surrounded by jagged rocks, still defended by a seventeenth-century citadel. The house of the Conde de Castro Guimarães, now a museum, contains some interesting pictures and a valuable library.

Leaving Lisbon by the Rua Joaquim Antonio de Aguiar, we pass the French Charles-Depierre Lycée, a magnificent building only recently completed. The next landmark on the road to Sintra consists of two aqueducts, one built in the seventeenth century called 'Aguas Libres', and the other modern, named after the Minister Duarte Pacheco. Our next stop is Queluz, an enchanting Baroque palace colour-washed in pink, once a royal residence built in imitation of Versailles. The French architect J.-B. Robillon and the Portuguese Mateus Vicente both worked on the building. Our most lasting impression is of the gardens and the ornamental lake of Neptune in front of the castle, and of the Staircase of the Lions climbing up under the trees. The interior reminds us more of Louis XV's rooms at Versailles than of the showy apartments of Louis XIV. The square-shaped 'Don Quixote's room' has a circular ceiling supported by columns. Probably it is in the Throne Room, with its cool harmony of mirrors and gilded wood, that we can most easily conjure up the ghosts of the court of Braganza. The unfortunate Queen Mariana, the charming Infanta who spent her childhood at Versailles and was betrothed to Louis XV, was destined to retire to this palace, modelled on the palaces of France, and exchange the pomp and ceremony of a court for the simple delights of a petty provincial home.

In the Serra da Sintra there are a number of delightful parks, such as the Quinta de Monserrate, scattered among the fragrant woods and the fountains gushing from the rocks. The town of Sintra boasts of three palaces. From the ruined Moorish castle there is a splendid view towards the Tagus and the sea. The castle of Pena, built on a rock by the Prince Consort Ferdinand of Coburg, is a bewildering mixture of every sort of style, a hotchpotch of Arab, Baroque and Manueline, though it derives a certain unity from the imaginative conception, not unworthy of a Cocteau, which animates the whole. Right in the centre of the town is the palace of Sintra, the greater part of which was built by John I and Manuel. The palace was used as a royal residence until the fall of the monarchy, and a number of delightful rooms are still shown to the public. The Sala dos Brasões, dating from the early seventeenth century, has walls lined with dazzling blue *azulejos*, and a ceiling in the form of an octagonal cupola bearing the arms of the principal noble families of Portugal. The Sala dos Cisnes, which derives its name from the swans painted on the ceiling, also has parti-coloured *azulejos* on the walls. But the most unforgettable feature of the palace is the great courtyard in the Moorish style, filled with the monotonous melancholy plash of a single slim fountain.

Mafra bears witness to King John V's love of pomp and splendour. This Baroque Escorial, built by the German Frederic Ludwig, extorts our reluctant admiration. The king's ambition here over-reaches itself, to the obvious detriment of one of the most perfect buildings in the whole peninsula. In spite of the many marvels of Mafra's palace-monastery, it remains a body without a soul. The façade, however, is undeniably impressive in its vitality and breadth of design. The library, in its breathless and somewhat insubstantial Baroque beauty, reminds one of the far superior library of Coimbra. There are some remarkable statues on the façade of the church. Nevertheless we are left with the painful impression of an ill-directed ambition, of a palace without a king and a monastery without monks.

A few miles away, on the coast north of Cabo Raso, the high flower-tufted cliffs of the port of Ericeira jut out over the sea.

Between Setubal and the south shore of the Tagus estuary, a small mountainous peninsula, dominated by the Serra da Arrabida, offers some of the most entrancing scenery in Portugal, with the charm of one of the Balearic Islands transported to the Atlantic. The cape of Espichel rises close to a perfect, sandy cove, and has an old pilgrimage shrine standing at the back of a vast dilapidated square. From the battlements of the fortress of Sesimbra a view can be obtained of the port of Setubal, with the fishing-boats drawn up on the beach as at Nazaré. From Formosinho the view extends to the estuary of the Tagus and the Atlantic to the south, and embraces the entire peninsula and the surrounding waters. The coast road to Portinho de Arrabida and Setubal, which runs along glaring cliffs through enchanted woods filled with the fragrance of sea and flowers, passes the Convento Novo clinging to the hillside like a bunch of white lilac gleaming under the shadow of the cypresses. Finally we reach the heights above the entry to the bay of Setubal, whose bed is visible beneath the blue transparent water, as if the weary earth had anticipated the Day of Judgment and were resting quietly in the sight of its Maker.

The big fishing port of Setubal, with its peaceful quays and dazzling white straight streets which remind us of Africa, boasts of one famous building, the Manueline Church of Jesus built by Boytac. The near-by fortress of Palmela and the gardens of the palace of Bacalhoa bring our excursion south of the Tagus to a happy end.

Along the north shore of the Tagus estuary the road to Santarem runs monotonously through an uninteresting industrial area: the only redeeming features of a long and dusty drive is an occasional glimpse of the river enlivened by the painted sails of the fishing-boats. At Vila Franca de Xira, a popular bull-fighting centre, we cross over south by the Marshal

Carmona bridge, the only bridge between Vila and the estuary. The road to Santarem runs through a green stretch of undulating wooded country. The town, perched picturesquely on a hill north of the river, was once a royal residence and still contains many notable works of art, though much has unfortunately been destroyed. The fountain dates from the fourteenth century: the church of the da Graça monastery is in the Gothic style of Batalha. Of earlier date is the convent of São Francisco, now a barracks. The formal beauty of the façade of the seminary, once the Jesuit College, has often been reproduced in South America. The Romanesque and Gothic church of São João de Alporão, one of whose towers was demolished in 1785 to make way for Maria I's coach, is now a museum: it contains the Flamboyant tomb of Duarte de Meneses. The body of this heroic knight was mutilated by the Moors, and the sole surviving relic, consisting of a single tooth, was buried in the tomb by his widow.

Instead of following the road to Abrantes, we will now cross the Tagus by the bridge at the foot of the hill of Santarem, and make our way through the province of Ribatejo in the direction of Evora.

There is nothing to interest in the towns—Almeirim, Salvatierra de Magos, Benavente—but the country has a tranquil beauty and unexpected charm, while the damp level plain forms a contrast to the mountainous scenery which has accompanied our journey from the Minho. Now we are faced with a vast green expanse of rice-fields and meadows and saturated fields, a world still sodden with the moisture of the Tagus. The roads are dykes, covered in flowers and bordered with eucalyptus, tamarisks and agaves. Against the alternately pale blue or blazing sky, we make out the shapes of the trees before we can distinguish their colours. Every now and then a pine-wood engulfs us beneath its shuddering pointed branches: we might be the first living creatures to disturb the unbroken silence. Flocks of sheep and herds of black pigs wander over the fields. The men wear a curious kind of green bonnet with a red stripe. A solitary horseman appears in the distance: it is Don Quixote, lost in the Ribatejo, wearing his voluminous cloak and filthy warm sheepskin with a dignity no disillusion will ever shake. A family of storks flap by against the brilliant blue of the sky filtering through the leafy trees.

94. VILA FRANCA DI XIRA
LE PONT MARÉCHAL CARMONA
THE MARSHAL CARMONA BRIDGE

95. LISBONNE DEPUIS LE TAGE.
LISBON FROM THE TAGUS.

LISBONNE.
LISBON.

96. VARINAS.

97. CASA DOS BICOS.

98. PRAÇA DOS RESTAURADORES.

99. LA CATHÉDRALE.   LISBONNE.   100. ÉGLISE DES CARMES.
THE CATHEDRAL.   LISBON.   CARMELITE CHURCH.

ATEAU
NT-
RGES.
SAINT-
RGES
TLE.

BONNE.
BON.

RUE
FAMA.
REET
HE
MA.

102

103 à 104. LISBONNE. DANS L'ALFAMA.
LISBON. IN THE ALFAMA.

105.
LISBONNE.
LE PORT.
LISBON.
THE HARBOUR.

106.
LISBONNE.
LA TOUR DE BELEM.
LISBON.
THE BELEM TOWER.

107-108. LA TOUR DE BELEM. DÉTAILS.
DETAILS FROM THE BELEM TOWER.

COUVENT DES HIÉRONYMITES.
MONASTERY OF THE HIERONYMITES.

LISBONNE.
LISBON.

DÉTAIL DE FAÇADE.
DETAIL FROM FAÇADE.

LISBONNE
LISBON.

III.
CLOÎTRE DU COUVENT
DES HIÉRONYMITES.
CLOISTER OF THE
HIERONYMITES MONASTERY.

113-114.
LISBONNE. MUSÉE D'ART ANCIEN.
LISBON. MUSEUM OF ANCIENT ART.

CRISTOVÃO DE MORAES. PORTRAIT DU ROI DOM SEBASTIÃO.
PORTRAIT OF THE KING DOM SEBASTIÃO.

114.
DOMINGOS VIEIRA.
PORTRAIT D'ISABEL
DE MOURA.
PORTRAIT OF ISABEL
DE MOURA.

115 à 119. LISBONNE. MUSÉE D'ART A[NCIEN]
LISBON. MUSEUM OF ANCIE[NT ART]

116. CHEVALIER À LA LANCE.
KNIGHT WITH SPEAR.

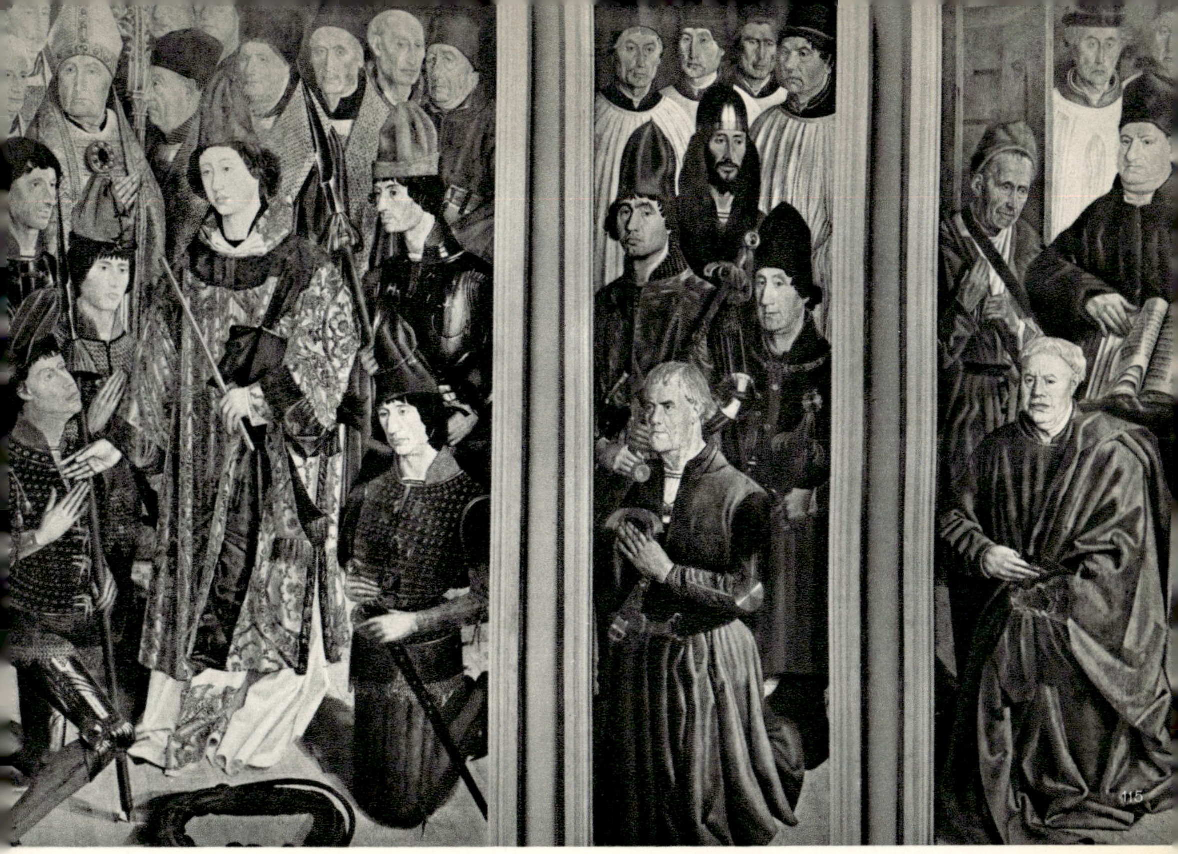

115

UE DE NUNO GONÇALVES.
E BY NUNO GONÇALVES.

117. VOLET DES PÊCHEURS. DÉTAIL.
SIDE-PANNEL SHOWING THE FISHERMEN. DETAIL.

117

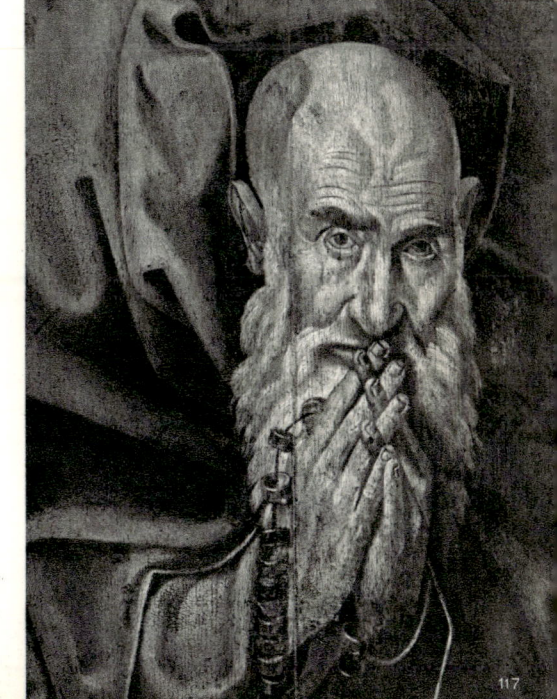

POLYPTIQUE DE
NUNO CONÇALVES.

RETABLE BY
NUNO CONÇALVES.

PÊCHEURS.
FISHERMEN.

119. SAINT-VINCENT.
ST. VINCENT.

120. AZULEJOS DE L'ÉGLISE SÃO VICENTE DE FORA.
     AZULEJOS IN THE SÃO VICENTE DE FORA CHURCH.
121. PARC DU CHÂTEAU DE QUELUZ.
     THE PARK OF QUELUZ CASTLE.
122. SINTRA. LE CHÂTEAU DE LA PENA.
     THE PENA CASTLE.

123-124. À SESIMBRA.
AT SESIMBRA.

125. SETÙBAL.

126. VILA FRANCA DE XIRA.
LES CAMPINOS DU RIBATEJO.
THE CAMPINOS OF THE RIBATEJO.

127 à 134. VILA FRANCA DE XIRA.
COURSES DE TAUREAUX.
BULL-FIGHTING.

128

129

130

132

CHAPTER V

Evora and the Alentejo

On leaving Portugal, the traveller will bring away with him memories which up to now we ourselves have shared: enjoyable memories of a populous countryside covered with green fields and woods and hills. A very different aspect is presented by the Alentejo. Consisting of two provinces—Alto Alentejo with its capital Evora, and Baixo Alentejo with its capital Beja—it occupies about a third of the whole country. It is a vast plain which might be part of Castile, flat and monotonous, white under the hot sunshine, with here and there a gentle rise and fall to emphasize the majesty of the scene. Under an incomparable sky the empty but cultivated fields stretch away, with flocks of sheep shepherded by a patriarch who might have stepped out of the Bible. In summer the earth is roasted by the sun, and the peasants protect themselves with layers of woollens. Villages are few and far between; the big farms, or *montes*, remind us of the Gallo-Roman *villas*—and indeed there are many reminders of the Roman occupation in this part of the country; for instance, the two provincial capitals were called Liberalitas Julia and Pax Julia. The towns, with their houses chequered snow-white and black in the sun and shade, look like great clusters of almond blossom.

Quitting the river Tagus region we cross an interminable tract of desert. In this noble and naked district the shades of green are infinite in variety, the clumps of trees imprint their sharp outlines on the featureless land, and a straight, almost African road leads us into the peace of the Alentejo.

For a long time our course lies to the south-east. A halt at Montemor-o-novo, and the level plain resumes once more: then in the distance appears the white and radiant town of Evora.

The town is built on a shelf of rock, but the mountains are far away on the horizon, and the country before us resembles the Beauce district of

France forming a humble approach to Chartres Cathedral. The cathedral of Evora rises above a mass of whitewashed buildings, belfries, monasteries, palaces and walls. The old streets are a treasure-store of art, the crowded squares are those of an ancient market town; and it is in this blend of fine art and peasant vigour that the uniqueness of Evora consists.

The town has a long and fascinating history. It prospered in Roman times, was fortified by the Visigoths, and occupied by the Arabs after the battle of Guadalete. In 1165 it was recaptured from the infidels by the renowned general, Geraldo Sempavor, and handed back to King Afonso Henriques. Soon afterwards it became the seat of the Military Order of St Benedict of Calatrava and a royal residence: King Afonso III, King Diniz and King Afonso IV all lived here. It was at Evora that an army was raised to succour Alfonso XI of Castile and to rout the Moslems at the battle of Salado in 1340. Under the Aviz dynasty this 'noble and ever loyal city' acquired a status of great importance, ranking second to Lisbon; and thanks to the presence of the monarchs, enjoyed a golden age of art and letters. Under King Manuel and King John III many splendid buildings were erected, and there was a brilliant period of humanism to which Portuguese scholars still look wistfully back. Mention must be made among others of the chroniclers Duarte Galvão and Garcia de Resende, of Bishop Afonso de Portugal and of Cardinal Afonso, King Manuel's son. At the Renaissance, Jean Petit and Gil Vicente shed lustre on the town. The Jesuit University was founded after the death of John III, and King Sebastian lived in Evora for five years after 1560. On 21st August 1637, during the period of Spanish occupation, Manuelinho's rising gave the first signal for the restoration of national independence. In the following century the Jesuit University was unfortunately suppressed by Pombal. In 1808 Loison's troops captured and sacked the town, which only escaped complete disaster thanks to the courage of the archbishop.

Today, Evora retains the character of a secluded agricultural town, attracting the lover of art not only by its still intact and wonderful buildings but by the unfailing picturesqueness of its narrow, tortuous streets winding up between mysterious walls overhung with flowers. There is poetry in

Evora and the Alentejo

the very names of these alleys: Arras do Cardeal (The Cardinal's Nurses), Cosinha de Sua Altesa (His Highness's Kitchen), Escudeiro da Roda (The Squire of the Wheel), or simply Odreiros (The Leather Bottle Merchant). And whenever the street opens into a tiny square the sun blazes down with an African violence.

Within these privileged walls art was never at a loss for a patron, and every period is represented. Roman remains include the sculptures in the museum, the triumphal arch which once stood in the Geraldo Square, and above all the Temple of Diana, resting like a seagull in the sun. The Goths have left us the greater part of the walls and the towers which defended the original enceinte. Practically no Arab buildings survive, but there are still many medieval remains, such as part of the cathedral walls and, from John II's reign, the church of the Loios and the chapel of São Bras, the latter completed by King Manuel. Every reign provides an illustration of the succession of styles. With the Arruda brothers and Nicolas Chanterène, in the reign of John III, there was an incomparable outburst of Renaissance building—we need mention only the Graça Church, the palace of Melo, the fountain of the Portas de Moura and the Geraldo Square. At the beginning of the sixteenth century Frei Carlos was painting in his convent of Espinheiro. The fortifications in the style of Vauban were built by French engineers in the seventeenth century.

Let us now wander at will through the town. In the centre, the noisy bustling Praça do Geraldo, partially lined by arcades, is strung out like a rosary with the capitals of the columns for beads. In the square is an Estremoz marble fountain erected in 1571 by King Sebastian's master-architect, Afonso Alvares. To make room for it the Roman triumphal arch was demolished: the bronze crown on the top was a tribute from the Senate of Evora to Philip II (1583). On this spot there stood formerly the early sixteenth-century town hall and the royal palace of the second dynasty. At one end of the square stands the church of Santo Antão, consecrated in 1563, a rather heavy example of Portuguese Baroque. In contrast with the urban animation of the Praça do Geraldo, the Cathedral Square is the artistic centre of Evora. Facing a vista of gardens and open country the columns of the Temple of Diana (there is no proof of any connection with the goddess) rise up in the silent air. Close at hand are the museum, formerly the archbishop's palace, containing a fine collection of paintings and sculpture; the palace of the Inquisition and the palace of the Inquisitors, the choir school, and finally the cathedral itself to complete an astonishing ensemble.

The cathedral is one of the most remarkable in the whole of Portugal. Founded in 1186, it is of granite, with a tower resembling the *cimborios* of Salamanca and Zamora, and is a blend of Romanesque and Gothic, such as we often find in Portugal. The greater part was built in the time of Bishop Durando Pais and King Afonso III. To the reign of Afonso IV belong the south side of the transept, the cloister, and probably the statues on the porch, among which is a particularly striking group of the Apostles—healthy Alentejo peasants, including a St Peter with an enormous nose, to represent the sturdy fishermen of Galilee. In its ensemble the building is obviously comparable with the cathedrals of Coimbra and Lisbon, while the cloister is modelled on the cloister at Alcobaça. Thanks to the generosity of John V, the choir was rebuilt by Ludwig between 1718 and 1740: it is one of the many splendid products of that period, exhibiting a marked contrast between its marbles and the severity of the granite. The cathedral boasts of at least two admirable sculptures: the fifteenth-century polychrome stone *Virgin of O* and a *St Gabriel* attributed to Olivier de Gand. Among many other interesting features are a Renaissance pulpit (1570) and the Capela do Esperão with a retable of the *Descent from the Cross* by Pedro Nunes (1620). The Treasury contains an ivory Virgin which opens out into a triptych, a silver-gilt reliquary cross with lustrous enamels, and numerous pieces of sixteenth- and seventeenth-century plate.

The Regional Museum contains the remarkable tombs of Alvarez de Costa and Afonso of Portugal by Chanterène, who also sculpted the columns from the Paraiso Monastery and the choir window from the church of the Convento da Graça. Its principal attraction, however, is the paintings. These include the retable of the old choir of the cathedral, probably painted in Evora by a group of Flemish artists, which represents the life of Mary; a *Virgin in Glory Crowned by Angels*, betraying the influence of Gérard David; and several smaller pictures obviously influenced by Hugo van der Goes. There are many other attractive works, as for instance a seventeenth-century *Holy Family* by Joseph de Obidos: the Infant Jesus is saying grace, Joseph and Mary are sitting down to dinner, and the familiar domestic scene is full of religious feeling and delicate poetry.

Many other buildings are well worth a visit: the monastery of the Loios (named after the canons of the Order of St Eligius) and its church, cloister and chapter-house, the university with its cloister reminding us of Coimbra, the palace of the Counts of Basto; but we must hurry on. The Largo das Portas de Moura remains in the memory perhaps even longer than the Cathedral Square and its surroundings: it is a circus of white buildings which include the façades of the Convento do Carmo and the palace of the Cordovils, and a fountain dating from 1556 surmounted by an armillary sphere, the whole ensemble forming a perfect and unforgettable picture. The semi-ruined Convento de Graça, now used as a barracks, used to belong to the Order of St Augustine: the work of rebuilding was entrusted by John III to Miguel de Arruda, Diogo de Torralva, Manuel Pires and Nicolas Chanterène. Some of the sculptures have been transferred to the museum; some of the statues on the façade of the church are not unworthy of Michelangelo. Among other fine buildings may be mentioned the church of the convent of São Francisco, a curious mixture of Gothic and Moorish architecture with its Casa dos Ossos, a chapel lined with bones in the morbid taste fairly common in Portugal; the church of São Bras, whose battlements and pepperpot turrets make it look like a fortress; the gate of the Cemetery dos Remedios by Chanterène; the convent of Santa Clara, home of the Beltraneja, the unfortunate rival of Isabella the Catholic for the throne of Castile; and in the public gardens the defaced remains of the palaces of King Duarte and Bishop Afonso de Portugal. Evora blends all its churches and houses into one sovereign harmony in which every vibrating note contributes to one inspired chord: for centuries this splendid city of thinkers and artists has basked in the rays of the sun.

Nor does this radiance come only from the sun: it radiates into the environs, where we can inspect the seventeenth-century charterhouse, the Gothic and Renaissance monastery of São Bento de Castris, the convent of Espinheiro, and the enchanting little circular Renaissance temple of the Bom Jesus at Valverde, all of which awaken memories of Evora's glorious past.

Continuing our way across the splendid monotony of the endless plain, we come to Vila Vicosa which, in addition to the imposing enceinte of its ancient fortress, has a fine open square on which stands the palace of the dukes of Braganza. Behind its architectural façade the great staircase and the ceilings of some of the rooms are decorated with early seventeenth-century frescoes in the Italian style; of earlier date is the charming Manueline cloister. The rooms contain the possessions handed down from generation to generation by the house of Braganza. The Aubusson and Brussels tapestries (particularly a sixteenth-century *Descent from the Cross* and *Story of Achilles*) and the Italian Renaissance pottery are of only minor interest: far more remarkable is the reliquary of the Holy Rood, studded with precious stones, made by Felipe de Vallejo in the second half of the seventeenth century. The private apartments of King Carlos and Queen Amelia bear witness to the homely family life of the last days of the monarchy: there are pictures by the king, who was a gifted landscape painter; photographs of court functions; and some furniture, often in poor taste. The collections of weapons and the kitchens with their amazing battery of copper utensils bring our visit to an end on a picturesque note.

The sixteenth-century convent of Chagas in the palace square contains the tombs of the dukes of Braganza, and the ducal pantheon is in the church of the Agostinhos. The near-by Gate of Knots is a reminder of the charm of Manueline art.

As we move eastward towards Spain the country becomes more mountainous, and we come upon a succession of frontier towns, all much alike, whose history recalls the age-long rivalry between Castile and Portugal. Their repeated appearance soon becomes monotonous: each

Evora and the Alentejo

one of them clinging to its hillside presents the same white buildings under the same blue sky, and none has anything unique to detain the traveller. At Borba the doors and windows of the houses are framed in blue and red. A little farther on Estremoz offers some typical pottery, including the parti-coloured vases sprouting stone flowers. This old town, at the top of a hill reached through steep and intricate valleys, has a lordly keep and a palace in which Queen St Isabella died. Elvas, the scene of many meetings between the Kings of Spain and Portugal, has a few old churches, together with a Manueline cathedral and yet another fortress. Portalegre is rich in Baroque palaces, like that of the Abrançalhas which dates from the seventeenth century and has wrought-iron windows: the old monastery of Conceiçáo contains the tomb of Jorge de Melo by Nicolas Chanterène. Still farther north Castelho de Vide has some old doors in its steep and narrow streets, and fine views over the picturesque countryside.

But our real destination is Beja, that remote town in the south famous for the story of the Portuguese nun. According to tradition it was in the old convent of Conceição that Sor Mariana Alcoforado fell in love with the Chevalier de Chamilly during the Spanish wars in the reign of Louis XIV, and after his return to France wrote him the five famous letters, justly acclaimed as a masterpiece. The town, unfortunately, hardly lives up to this story of an unhappy love-affair. Beja is only a small, drowsy country town, the convent is now a museum, and the window high up in the cloister may or may not have been the window of Sor Mariana's cell. Still, the museum is worth a short visit, with its chapel reminding us of Batalha and containing some charming pieces of local sculpture. Other objects of interest are the fifteenth-century civil hospital, the keep of King Diniz and the Visigothic church of Santo Amoro. Nevertheless, as we watch the ox-wagons lumbering through the quiet streets under the stifling heat of the sun, we cannot help wondering whether it was really in Beja that Sor Mariana's strange passion burned unrequited for so many wasted years.

But we must now follow the call of the south, the lure of Africa. Avoiding the direct route, we make our way to the Atlantic coast across the Serra de Grandola. On the heights the tall green grass shivers in the evening wind, the flowers increase as we descend the slopes, and presently São Tiago de Cacém comes into sight. The *pouseda*, or government inn, admirably situated, awaits us, all around is a tender blue and green, and the whole countryside is a preparation for tomorrow's discovery—the Algarve.

135. VUE SUR EVORA
VIEW OF EVORA

EVORA. LA CATHÉDRALE.
THE CATHEDRAL.

136. LA TOUR LANTERNE.
THE LANTERN TOWER.

137. LE TRIFORIUM.
THE TRIFORIU[M]

138. APÔTRES.　　　EVORA. PORCHE DE LA CATHÉDRALE.
　　　APOSTLES.　　　　　THE CATHEDRAL PORCH.

139. SAINT-PIERRE.
　　　ST. PETER.

EVORA.
140. VUE SUR LE TEMPLE DE DIANE.
VIEW OF THE TEMPLE OF DIANA.

141. COUVENT DE SÃO FRANCISCO.
LA CASA DOS OSSOS.
THE SÃO FRANCISCO CONVENT.
THE CASA DOS OSSOS.

142. À ELVAS.
AT ELVAS

143. VILA VIÇOSA.
PORTE DES NŒUDS.
GATE OF KNOTS.

144. MAISON D'ALENTEJO.
A HOUSE IN THE ALENTEJO.

145. À PORTALEGRE.
AT PORTALEGRE.

146-147. EN ALENTEJO.
IN ALENTEJO.

SALLES DU COUVENT DE CONCEIÇÃO DEVENU MUSÉE RÉGIONAL.
ROOMS IN THE CONCEIÇÃO CONVENT, NOW THE LOCAL MUSEUM.

CHAPTER VI

The Algarve

LEAVING São Tiago de Cacém, we proceed on our way towards the Algarve, Portugal's African fringe. Even before the scenery changes we find outselves looking out for the first sign that we are entering this new and legendary province. This region on the Atlantic coast, 90 miles long and 30 miles broad, has often been referred to, with more or less justification, as a strip of Africa which has strayed into Portugal. Wave after wave the rounded mountain-tops stretch into the horizon; valleys and slopes are perpetually gay with flowers; the whitewashed houses stand out sharply against the immaculate sky; the gaunt serrated chimneys lift an unexpected finger to the sky; the country is a boundless orchard of fig-trees, almond-trees, agaves and many other exotic species, sloping down to a sea that is almost always calm.

On the opposite coast is Muslim Africa, of which the Algarve was once an integral part, and which has left an indelible mark on the houses and customs and even the scenery of the province.

In fact, the legendary reputation of this province, like a desert mirage, has invested it with a beauty to which it cannot perhaps lay claim: its real charm is not indeed inferior, but simply different.

The province brings no sudden revelation of an unknown aspect of Portugal: in every other province we have encountered, even if only in rough sketch, the features for which the Algarve is celebrated. It may be an orchard *par excellence*, it may have built more 'cubical cities' under the blazing sun, it may preserve a stronger flavour of the Muslim occupation; but all the same it is not yet Africa. Rather is it a dream of Africa, remembered by Portugal amid her valleys fragrant with flowers and her now fertile fields, as she contentedly faces her old enemy across the peaceful sea. Moreover, the Algarve, though undeniably beautiful, lacks that magical 'something' that fires the imagination in the region between Douro

150. VERS BEJA
    TOWARDS BEJA

and Minho: above all, thanks to the earthquakes, it lacks interesting buildings.

For a little while longer our road winds among the gentle slopes of the Alentejo hills, from which we are surprised to see the dark green trees sticking up like the knob of a gatepost. Beyond the Serra de Cercal the country grows barer. Here and there appear glistening patches of red earth, and for long stretches the soil is covered by a damp velvet coat of grass stirring timidly in the wind.

As we advance farther south the mountains follow one another in quicker succession, and the valleys are carpeted with rock-roses. We pass the heights of the Serra de Monchique on our left and arrive in Aljezur, whose bright houses are dominated by a ruined castle.

We are now approaching Lagos and the Algarve's wonderful coast. The mountains grow larger, the multiple shades of green blend in an entrancing symphony, the fig-trees bloom on every side, and Lagos appears gleaming white on the shore of her bay, close to the blue Atlantic reflecting the blue sky.

The bay extends for more than a mile between the Ponta dos Tres Irmãos and the Ponta da Piedade; from here, in the fifteenth and sixteenth centuries, many maritime expeditions put to sea.

The town has few good buildings. The Manueline window of the hospital from which King Sebastian addressed his troops is of more historical than artistic interest. On the other hand, the commonplace façade of the church of São Antonio conceals an unexpected and teeming world of gilded *boiserie*. Flights of angels flit among the Solomonic columns of the high altar, gathering the grapes for the consecrated wine. In the midst of this amusing, bustling throng, St Anthony lies stretched in his lofty cell. Under the gallery stands the Virgin, also in gilded wood. There is a dummy ceiling in the Italian style whose ornamental colonnades are admirably in keeping with this animated scene, bursting with the creatures of the sculptor's fancy. In the statuettes of the side-aisles his imagination is allowed to run riot: in the place of caryatides we have romping angels—or perhaps we should call them Cupids—mounted on mythical monsters and waving garlands. The artist is not afraid of a

The Algarve

picturesque scene: a fight between two knights, a stag hunt, fishermen at their nets and peasants bleeding a pig.

Between Lagos and Cape St Vincent there are about 25 miles of the most attractive coastline in the Algarve. Just outside the town is the Ponta da Piedade: the sea has partially destroyed and submerged the foot of the cape, peeling the vegetation from the tall cliffs and encircling the worn rocks with its dazzling waves. From the headland we seem to be looking at a ruined amphitheatre stripped and battered by the sea, pitted with caves and washed by the Atlantic pounding eternally on the flower-strewn coast.

From the little watering-place of Luz de Lagos we can make out the promontories of Sagres and Cape St Vincent on one side, and the bay of Lagos and the heights of the Serra de Monchique on the other. Continuing farther westwards, we approach the farthermost point of Portugal—and of Europe.

The road is bordered with agaves, aloes and palm-trees. Masses of geraniums hang from the white walls of the houses to the ground, or swell into blazing bushes in the wayside fields. The clear green meadows are dotted with almond-trees, and the blossom of the fig-trees sweeps the ground and hides their trunks from view: the whole earth is strewn with innumerable little mounds of leaves.

The sky and the sea, the fields and the flowers all seem to belong to a world apart, a world ignorant of sin and the Fall, which since man was created has known nothing but the perpetual peace of springtime. Surely this innocent lost paradise is not the world of men for whom Christ suffered and died? The tragic story of Christianity becomes irrelevant in the midst of this incredible and unforgettable foaming sea of fig-trees and geraniums.

Nevertheless, at the end of a lane as thick with flowers as the fields, set in gently undulating country, a chapel appears in sight: it is Nossa Senhora de Guadeloupe. This exquisite thirteenth-century Romanesque building has the shape of a sturdy though slightly bent old peasant woman: its rough sandstone columns and capitals have a primitive and brutal beauty. Its very presence here provokes surprise: a rustic sanctuary, the product of artistic rather than religious inspiration, a flower of the field blossoming in a lost valley lulled to sleep by the sound of the sea.

In Raposeira we encounter for the first time the memory of Henry the Navigator. Next comes Vila do Bispo, set in the verdant hills, which we enter through rows of houses smothered in geraniums. Windmills turn briskly in the breeze. Banks of flowers rise at our feet. But once the village is passed, we cross a wild plateau lashed by the wind from the open sea, and our enchanted lost paradise gives way to a grandiose landscape dark with forebodings of the end of the world. Yet even here nature rebels against such austerity, and summer strews the ground once more with the eternal geraniums.

The rocky promontory of Sagres is pierced by two chimneys, down which the golden-blue sea rushes with a shattering din: towards the west, across a bay, looms Cape St Vincent. Seen from a distance, with its relatively flat top rising high above the sea, it looks like the gigantic back of some prehistoric marine monster, stranded here thousands of years ago. The scenery unites grandeur to exquisite charm; the plateau between Sagres and the Cape is spangled with flowers. We now approach the outbuildings of the lighthouse towering above the Cape; the sea is wonderfully calm, and the soaring gulls and the many passing ships lessen the feeling of being alone on a deserted promontory.

Many ships have sailed these waters: here Tourville and Nelson triumphed, and to this spot the body of St Vincent was brought before being conveyed to Lisbon. But the place is haunted above all by the memory of Henry the Navigator. His name reminds us that we have not only reached the last corner of Portugal projecting into the sea, but that we are standing on the threshold of that second and boundless maritime kingdom won by the voyages of discovery and bequeathed to his country by the great Infante.

After all the beauty of the orchard of the Algarve, the finishing stroke is given by Cape St Vincent, standing majestically at the centre of 25 miles of flowers and sea. But we must first take a look at the coast which stretches east of Lagos up to the Spanish frontier. The houses look like bouquets of white roses in full bloom. The road ascends to disclose a vast panorama of wonderful colours, with the fringe of the ever-present sea in the distance.

The coast has a number of charming bays and picturesque rocks, of fascinating villages and houses with serrated chimneys. Passing quickly through the port of Portimão we reach the near-by resort of Praia da Rocha. In the summer months two motionless features can be distinguished on the russet sands of the beach: the high copper-coloured rocks fashioned by the sea through the centuries into fantastic piles of ruins, and the gaudy tents waiting in the windless air for the bathers. Punctually between the hours of eleven and one o'clock they make their appearance on the still, sun-drenched scene, like homing swallows or swarming bees. At the appointed hour the beach, which up to now has moved us with the formal beauty of a painting, comes to life with the confused shimmer of glistening bodies and the hum of human voices.

Inland, the Serra de Monchique is a blaze of mimosa, rhododendrons and arbutus interspersed with pines, cork-oaks and chestnut-trees: the wild valleys blossom out into meadows, and at every turn in the road the sea is hidden from view.

To the north we mount to the spa of Caldas de Monchique crouching in its ravine. All around are broad panoramas unrivalled by any save the view from Bussaco. The trees climb up the terraced slopes, and from beyond the hills, humped like mole-hills, the Algarve gazes into her favourite mirror—the sea.

Ascending still higher to 1,640 feet, we come to the little town of Monchique, with its Manueline church door, its ruined monastery of Nossa Senhora do Desterro, its terraces smothered in camellias, and on either side the highest points in the province, the peaks of La Foia and La Picota. From the chestnut groves of the latter can be seen, far off to the west, the capes of Sagres and St Vincent, and a last sight of the sparkling sea, stretching to the horizon and the promise of the ocean beyond. Our last halt is Saboia, which we reach by a road running between savage precipices and hanging gardens, over vast plateaux or through narrow defiles, a rare combination of wildness and charm.

Silves, to the east, was once the provincial capital, and after the reconquest was endowed with one of the finest Gothic cathedrals in the district: its pale reddish stone is like sun-ripened fruit. The red sandstone Moorish castle has preserved its circular way and its cistern, and still keeps watch over the town.

Descending from Monchique, we now follow the coastal road which runs to Faro, and affords only an occasional glimpse of the vast panoramas we have left behind. Our way lies through an endless orchard, with the white villages dotted among luxuriant vegetation.

Loulé, slightly to the north, contains a few interesting buildings, notably a thirteenth-century church; but its main charm resides in its Oriental atmosphere, the gardens with their profusion of flowers and trees, the rough-cast white houses, the pierced chimneys, and the terraces from which one may watch the Battle of Flowers at Carnival-time. Quitting this scene from the *Arabian Nights,* we are amazed to find ourselves back again in the eighteenth century, in the palace and gardens of Estoi: at Milreu, not far away, there are some Roman remains.

Faro itself, the capital of the province, is an uninteresting fishing-port and commercial centre whose religious buildings, particularly the cathedral, were badly damaged in the earthquake of 1755. In an old cemetery near the Carmo Church there is a chapel entirely lined with bones, in the morbid taste displayed in other Portuguese churches.

Olhão, another port, has been nicknamed the 'cubical town' because of the peculiar shape of its snow-white stone houses.

After a visit to Tavira's Gothic church of Santa Maria de Castelo, we yield to the lure of the frontier and push on to the Guadiana, whose left bank is in Spain. In Vila Real de San Antonio, on the west bank of the river's mouth opposite the Andalusian town of Ayamonte, we experience for the last time the spell of Portugal. The town was built by the great Minister Pombal in conformity with his usual rectilinear plan. Its principal industry of tunny-fishing provides the visitor with a unique spectacle of beauty combined with violence.

The fish, weighing seven or eight hundred pounds, swim regularly in shoals towards the Mediterranean. Since they always hug the coast, the tunny-fishers employ a *madrague,* a complicated contrivance consisting of a series of nets which the fish cannot possibly break through. The first barrier intercepts the tunny and deflects them into the 'death chamber'. Here they rise to the surface and are slowly hauled towards the shore. This majestic spectacle now gives place to a veritable fight to the death. The fishermen hang on with one hand to the ropes, and by means of a small harpoon strapped to the other wrist force the fish to leap into the boats. Sometimes they even dive off the boats into the sea and engage in a desperate duel. Meanwhile the fish strike out blindly, leaping and struggling in the net, and sooner or later succumb to their wounds and collapse in the bottom of the boats.

This furious fight continues for a long time, until at last nothing remains but the stench of carnage to poison the peaceful evening, and a purple veil floating on the surface of the sea where the rays of the setting sun mingle with the blood of the slaughtered fish.

151. LAGOS

152. DANS LA SERRA DE MONCHIQUE.
IN THE SERRA DE MONCHIQUE.

153. VILLAGE D'ALGARVE.
VILLAGE IN ALGARVE.

154 à 157.
RÉCOLTE DU LIÈGE DANS
LA SERRA DE MONCHIQUE
COLLECTING THE CORK IN
THE SERRA DE MONCHIQUE

158. CABO DE SAGRES.   159. PRAIA DA ROCHA.

. SAGRES.
VENDEUR D'EAU.
E WATER-SELLER.

161. FEMME DE TAVIRA.
WOMAN OF TAVIRA.

162-163. VILA REAL DE S. ANTONIO.
PÊCHE AU THON.
TUNNY FISHING.

162

164. TYPE DE PORTUGAIS.
A PORTUGUESE TYPE.

Conclusion

FLOWERS and green fields are not the whole of Portugal, though they may be one of its essential features. The main tourist routes cover the most populous, prosperous and smiling regions: hence the legend of the perpetual orchard which the traveller in Portugal expects to find. Nor are his hopes disappointed: how many times have we emerged from a valley to gaze in wonder at some landscape as beautiful as the Douro vineyards or the view from the Cruz Alta at Bussaco! Yet this is not the whole story; there is the poverty of the rocky soil hidden under the moss, the aridity of the mountain-tops looking down on the fertile valleys.

The mildness of this orchard-land is reflected in the character of the people: but here again there is another side to the picture. The cruelty of Inez de Castro's murderers and the savage revenge taken on them by Pedro the Cruel are as much a part of Portugal as the enchanting roads over the Serra da Arrabida.

The sea is never far off this narrow strip of land. The maritime discoveries taught the kingdom its true destiny, bringing it wealth and glory, and inspiring its great epic. But the hold of the land is equally strong, and Portugal is a land of peasants as well as of mariners.

There is thus a perpetual clash of interests, which in no way impairs the basic unity of the country, and is reflected in the Portugal of today. In the apparatus of a modern State provided by the Salazar régime, the humbler class—in contrast with a refined aristocracy and an advanced middle class in the Lisbon and Oporto regions—retains its primitive way of life. In the bright new post office a peasant will be struggling with a telegram form; past the gleaming petrol stations, gay with flowers, ride men and women in their traditional costumes to the immemorial rhythm of the lumbering ox-wagons. May it not be said that Portugal has one foot still in the Middle Ages, the other already in America?

165. PROCESSION

166-167. FÊTES.
FEASTS.

168. A PRAIA DE VIEIRA
AT PRAIA DE VIEIRA

The Kings and Queens of Portugal

DYNASTY OF BURGUNDY

Afonso Henriques (Afonso I)	1128–1185
Sancho I	1185–1211
Afonso II	1211–1223
Sancho II	1223–1248
Afonso III	1248–1279
Diniz (Denis I)	1279–1325
Afonso IV	1325–1357
Pedro I (Pedro the Cruel)	1357–1367
Fernão I (Ferdinand I)	1367–1383

DYNASTY OF AVIZ

João I (John I)	1385–1433
Duarte I (Edward I)	1433–1438
Afonso V	1438–1481
João II	1481–1495
Manuel I	1495–1521
João III	1521–1557
Sebastião I (Sebastian I)	1557–1578

DYNASTY OF BRAGANZA

João IV	1640–1656
Afonso VI	1656–1668
Pedro II	1683–1706
João V	1706–1750
José I (Joseph I)	1750–1777
Maria I	1777–1792
Regency of Prince João	1792–1816
João VI	1816–1826
Miguel I (Michael I)	1828–1834
Maria II	1834–1853
Pedro V	1855–1861
Luis I (Louis I)	1861–1889
Carlos I (Charles I)	1889–1908
Manuel II	1908–1910

Index

Abrantes, 179
Afonso, Cardinal, 222
Afonso, Infante, 46
Afonso Henriques (Afonso I), 15, 25, 44, 93, 124, 125, 163, 222, 266
Afonso II, 15, 266
Afonso III, 15, 163, 222, 224, 266
Afonso IV, 15, 167, 222, 224, 266
Afonso V, 17, 87, 89, 126, 127, 172, 266
Afonso VI, 18, 267
Afonso, Jorge, painter, 27
Afonso of Portugal, bishop, 25, 222, 224, 225
Africa, 14, 16, 17, 227, 245
Albujarrota, 16, 45, 125, 129, 168
Albuquerque, Afonso de, 17, 166
Alburitel, heath of, 124
Alcacer, 17
Alcacer-Kebir, 18, 171
Alcoa, river, 129, 131
Alcobaça, 16, 129. Monastery of Santa Maria, 21, 24, 26, 121, 125, 128, 129–31, 167, 170, 174, 175, 224, Nos. 80–2
Alcoforado, Sor Mariana, 227
Aleman, João, sculptor, 94
Alentejo district, 13, 28, 221–8, 246, Nos. 144, 146–7
Alexander VI, Pope, 17
Alfarrobeira, 17
Alfonso VI, of Leon, 15
Alfonso VII, of Leon, 15
Alfonso XI, of Castile, 222
Algarve, province of, 12, 14, 15, 228, 245–51, No. 153
Aljezur, 246
Almeida, Francisco de, 17
Almeida, Bishop Jorge d', 95
Almeida, José de, sculptor, 24, 26
Almeirim, 179
Alta Beira. *See* Beira
Alto Alentejo, province of, 221

Alvares, Afonso, architect, 223
Alvares Cabral, 17
Alvares Pereira, Constable Nuño, 16, 129, 168
Alvelos, Serra de, 121
Alvor, Counts of, 169
Amarante, Cruz, archbishop, 47
Amelia, Queen, 20, 166, 226
Anastasius IV, Pope, 96
Ança, 90
Andalusia, 250
Angola, 18, 20
Anthony of Padua, St, 98, 167
Arrabida, Serra da, 12, 178, 265
Arruda, Diogo de, architect, 22, 122, 123, 175, 223
Arruda, Francisco de, architect, 22, 123, 175, 223
Arruda, Miguel de, architect, 41, 123, 223, 225
Arzila, 17
Atlantic Ocean, 14, 44, 50, 88, 123, 162, 178, 245, 246
Aubusson tapestries, 43, 226
Augustine, Order of St, 225
Augustus, 14
Auvergne art, 20, 94
Aveiro, 28, 82, 89–90, Nos. 43–6
Averio, Duke of, 19
Aveiro, estuary of, 12, 88–90, Nos. 44–5
Avila, 85
Aviz dynasty, 16, 26, 127, 173, 222, 266. *See also* John I
Ayamonte, 250
Azambuja, Diogo de, 17, 90
Azores, 16

Baça, river, 129
Bacalhoa, 178
Baixa Beira. *See* Beira
Baixo Alentejo, province of, 221
Balearic Islands, 178
Barca d'Alva, 52

273

Barcelos, No. 39
Baroque art, 23, 26, 123, 170, 176, 177, 227
Barreiro, 162
Batalha, 124-9. Monastery of Our Lady of Victory, 22-3, 25, 121, 125-9, 168, 174, 175, 179, 227, Nos. 74-9
Beatrix, Queen, 16, 167
Beauce district, 221-2
Beira, provinces of, 12, 82, No. 61. Alta Beira, 13, 43 *note*, 82; Baixa Beira, 13, 82; Beira Litoral, 12, 43, 82, 121
Beja, 22, 221, 227, Nos. 148-50
Belem, 164, 173. Hieronymite monastery, 22, 99, 122, 123, 126, 128, 174-5, Nos. 109-12. Church, 25, 174. Tower, 22, 162, 175-6, Nos. 106-8
Beltraneja, the, 225
Benavente, 179
Benedict of Calatrava, Military Order of St, 222
Benlliure, architect, 86
Berlenga, island of, 132
Bernard, architect, 94, 167
Bertiandos, country house of Counts of, 47
Biscay, 23
Bom Jesus, temple of (Valverde), 226
Bom Jesus do Monte (Braga), 42, 47, No. 19
Bombay, 18
Borba, 227
Bordalo Pinheiro, R., 132
Bosch, Jerome, painter, 170
Bouchardon, sculptor, 164
Boytac, architect, 22, 84, 93, 126, 174, 178
Braga, 20, 28, 41, 44, 45-7, No. 19
Braganza, 42, Nos. 13, 20-5
Braganza, House of, 17, 18, 26, 42, 84, 163, 166, 170, 172, 177, 226, 267. *See also* John IV
Brazil, 17, 19, 24, 98
Bruges, Olivier de, painter, 95
Brussels tapestries, 43, 228
Burgundian dynasty, 131, 266. *See also* Henry of Burgundy
Bussaco, 99, 249, 265, No. 60

Cabo Raso, 178
Cabril gorge, 42
Caceres, 85
Cachão da Valeira, gorges of, 51
Cacilhas, 162
Cadiz, 170

Caesar, Julius, 163
Caldas de Monchique, 249
Caldas da Rainha, 132
Camoëns, poet, 16 *note*, 17, 92, 168, 175
Cantanhede, 90
Cântaro Magro, rocks of the, 86
Canterbury Cathedral, 126
Carlos, Don, 19
Carlos, Frei, painter, 27, 171, 223
Carlos I, 20, 164, 166, 226, 267
Carmona, Marshal, 20, 175
Carmona bridge, Marshal, 178-9, No. 94
Cascais, 162, 164, 174, 176
Castelho de Vide, 227
Castelo Bom, 83
Castelo Branco, 82, 85, No. 41
Castile, 11, 14, 16, 83, 221, 226
Castile, Constance of, 16
Castilho, Diogo de, architect, 25, 93
Castilho, João de, architect, 23, 122, 126, 174
Castro, Inez de, 15-16, 24, 84, 92, 265, No. 81
Castro, Machado de, sculptor, 23, 26, 164, 167, 169
Castro Guimares, Conde de, 176
Catalonia, 18
Catherine of Austria, 175
Catherine, Infanta, 18
Celorico da Beira, 85, 86
Celts, 28
Cercal, Serra de, 246
Ceuta, 16
Chamilly, Chevalier de, 227
Champaigne, Philippe de, painter, 173
Champnol, art of, 25, 174
Chanterène, Nicolas, architect and sculptor, 25, 26, 90, 93, 94, 97, 98, 174, 223, 224, 225, 227, No. 52
Charles II of England, 18
Charles V, Emperor, 123
Charterhouse, near Evora, 226
Chaves, 41, 43, No. 17
China, 17, 49
Churrigueras, the, architects, 24
Cistercians, 21, 121, 129, 131
Ciudad Rodrigo, 82-3
Clairvaux, art of, 129
Clement XI, Pope, 173
Clouet, François, painter, 50
Cluniac influence, 20

Index

Cocteau, Jean, writer, 177
Coelho, Pero, 16
Cogominho family, 44
Coimbra, 16, 25, 26, 45, 82, 90–9, 163, Nos. 11, 47–59. Arco de Almedina, 94. Avenida Sa da Bandeira, 94. *Cathedrals*: Romanesque (Sé Velha), 20, 24, 91, 94–5, 167, 224, Nos. 11, 47, 53; Sé Nova, 97. Colegio da Misericordia, 94. *Churches*: Santo Antonio dos Olivais, 98; São Bartolomeu, 93; Santa Clara a Velha, 131; San Salvador, 95; São Tiago, 93. Jardim da Manga, 94, 97; das Lágrimas, 92. *Monasteries*: Celas, 25, 95, 98; Santa Clara, 24, 91, 95–6, No. 56; Santa Cruz, 22, 25, 50, 93–4, 95, 97, 170, 174, No. 52. Machado de Castro Museum, 26, 91, 96, 96–7, Nos. 48, 55. Oratory of St Sebastian, 98. *Palaces*: Episcopal, 23, 94; Sub-Ripas, 94, No. 54. Portaferrea, 97, No. 49. *University*: 82, 91, 97–8, 163, 225, Nos. 49–51; Chapel, 22, 97; Library, 98, 177, No. 51; Paço das Escolas, 97, 98; Sala dos Capelos, 97; Via Latina, 97, No. 50
Coimbra, Pero de, sculptor, 24
Columbano, painter, 28, 167, 169
Columbus, Christopher, 17
Compostella, 47
Comprida, Lagoa, 86
Corgo gorge, 42
Cortes (of Coimbra), 16; (of Tomar), 18
Costa, Alvarez de, 25, 224
Cousinet, sculptor, 170
Cova da Iria, heath of, 124
Covadonga, 15
Covilha, 85
Cranach, Lucas, painter, 171
Cruz Alta of Bussaco, 99, 265

David, Gérard, painter, 170, 225
Dias, Bartolomeu, navigator, 17
Diniz (Denis I), 15, 83, 91, 222, 227, 266
Domingues, Afonso, architect, 125
Douradas. *See* Penhas
Douro, river, and its valley, 12, 13, 50–2, No. 37; Vineyards of, 44, 50–1, 265
Douro Litoral, province of, 13, 41, 48–50, 245
Duarte I, 16–17, 126, 127, 128, 225, 266
Dulce, Queen, 45
Dürer, Albrecht, 50, 93, 170

Egaz Moniz, 15
Egypt, 17
Eiffel, Gustave, 49
Eleanor, Queen, 16, 50
Eligius, Order of St, 225
Elvas, 227, No. 142
England, 16 *note*, 18, 19, 21, 49, 125–6, 169
Ericeira, 178
Erlon, Comte d', 130
Escorial, the, 23
Espichel, Cape, 12, 178
Espinheiro, Convent of, 223, 226
Espinho, Monte, 47
Estoi, 250
Estoril, 162, 164, 176
Estrêla, Serra da, 12, 85
Estremadura, province of, 13, 121
Estremoz, 223, 227
Evin, P.-A., 21
Evora, 20, 23, 27, 45, 179, 221–6, Nos. 135–41. *Alleys*: Arras do Cardeal, 223; Cosinho de Sua Altesa, 223; Escudeiro da Roda, 223; Odreiros, 223. Cathedral, 20, 23, 125, 167, 222, 224, Nos. 136–9. Cemetery dos Remedios, 225. *Churches*: of the Loios, 25, 223; Santo Antão, 223; São Francisco, 225, No. 141; São Bras, 223, 225. *Convents*: da Graça, 25, 223, 224, 225; Paraiso, 25, 224; des Loios, 25, 223; do Carmo, 225; Santa Clara, 225. *Museums*: of painting, and sculpture, 224; Regional, 224. *Palaces*: Melo, 223; of the Inquisition, 224; of the Inquisitors, 224; of the Counts of Basto, 225; of the Cordovils, 225. *Squares*: Praça do Geraldo, 223; Largo das Portas de Moura, 223, 225. Temple of Diana, 20, 223, No. 140. University, 222, 225
Evora, Fernão d', architect, 126
Eyck, Jan van, painter, 27, 173

Faro, 250
Farrobo, Conde de, 171
Fatima, 124, Nos. 69–72
Feirreirim, 43 *note*
Ferdinand, St, 127
Ferdinand I, 15, 16, 168, 266
Ferdinand of Coburg, Consort, 177
Fernandes, Garcia, painter, 27, 43 *note*
Fernandes, Mateus, architect, 22, 126, 127, Nos. 78–9

Fernandes, Vasco (the Great Vasco), 27, 43, 82, 87–8, 93, No. 10
Figueira da Foz, 90
Figueiredo, Cristovão de, painter, 27, 43 *note*, 93, 96, 132
Flemish School of painting, 27, 43, 49, 94, 95, 96, 171, 173, 224
Foia, La, mountain, 249
Fontes, Marquês de, 173
Fonfroide, 131
Formosinho, 178
France, French influence, 18, 19, 20, 23, 24, 27–8, 46, 94, 129, 169, 171, 223, 227
Franco, Francisco, sculptor, 26, 165
Fuentes de Oñoro, 83

Gabriel, architect, 164
Galicia, 11, 12, 15, 47
Galvão, Duarte, chronicler, 222
Gama, Vasco da, 17, 175
Gand, Jean de, painter, 95
Gand, Olivier de, sculptor, 122, 224
Garcia, Telo, sculptor, 24, 46
Garcia, Pero, sculptor, 46
Gens, St, bishop, 166
Geraldo, St, archbishop, 45
Germain brothers, goldsmiths, 170
Goa, 17
Godoy, 19
Goes, Hugo van der, painter, 225
Gomes, Gaspar and Fernão, painters, 27
Gonçalves, Alvaro, 16
Gonçalves, Nuno, painter, 26, 27, 90, 172, 173, 176, Nos. 115–19
Good Hope, Cape of, 17
Goths, 45, 86, 223
Goya, painter, 28, 171
Grandola, Serra de, 227–8
Greeks, 28
Greenland, 17
Guadalete, battle of, 222
Guadaloupe, 170
Guadiana, river, 13, 250
Guarda, 26, 83–5, No. 40
Guimarães, 15, 44–5, No. 18
Guinea, Gulf of, 16 17

Hapsburg, House of, 18
Henriques, Francisco, painter, 27, 85, 88
Henry II, 50, 83

Henry, Cardinal King, 18, 175
Henry of Burgundy, 15, 44
Henry the Navigator, 16, 127, 172, 173, 174, 248
Hodart, architect and sculptor, 25, 26, 97
Holland, and the Dutch, 18, 89
Hugo, Victor, 99
Huyghe, M. R., writer, 172
Huysmans, J. K., writer, 124

Iberians, 28
Ilhavo, 90
Indies, discovery and conquest of, 17, 89, 123, 163, 170
Infants. *See* Catherine; Ferdinand, St; Henry the Navigator; Isabella; John, Grand Master of Santiago; Peter, Regent
Irmãos, Ponta do Tres, 246
Isabella, St, consort of King Diniz, 24, 48, 91, 227
Isabella II, 19, 124
Isabella, Infanta, 27
Isabella the Catholic, 225
Isenbrandt, Andriaen, painter, 96
Italy, Italian influence, 24, 26, 27, 121, 169, 173, 225, 246

Japan, 17
Jesuits, 19
Jews, 17
Joãna, Princess Santa, 89
John I, of Castile, 16
John, Grand Master of Santiago, 127
John I (John of Aviz), 16, 17, 44, 45, 46, 124, 125, 126, 127, 177, 266
John II, 17, 87, 127, 167, 172, 173, 223, 266
John III, 17, 25, 27, 94, 126, 127, 167, 175, 222, 223, 225, 266
John IV, 18, 84, 267. *See also* Braganza, House of
John V, 19, 23, 24, 163, 169, 173, 177, 224, 267
John VI, 19, 267
John Franco, 20
Joseph I, 19, 23, 267
Junot, Marshal, 19

La Fontaine, writer, 166
Labrador, 17
Lagos, 16, 246–7, 248, No. 151

Index

Lambert, Elie, writer, 129
Lamego, 20, 42-3
Lancastrian line, 125. *See also* Philippa, Queen
Languedoc, influence of, 20. *See also* Boytac
Lanheses, 47
Lebrun, painter, 43
Leça do Bailo, 48
Leiria, 124, No. 73
Lena, river, 124, 125
Leo X, Pope, 168
Leon, 15
Leonor of Aragon, 22, 128, 132, 167, 168
Lima, bridge of, No. 28
Lima, river, 13, 47
Limoges enamels, 50, 87
Lisbon, 13, 19, 20, 27, 28, 85, 162-76, 222, 248, 265, Nos. 95-120. *Afama*, 167-8, Nos. 102-4; São Miguel, 168; Bicha Alley, 168. Ajuda Park, 173. Alamada de D. Henriques, 166. Arsenal do Exercito, 167. Avenida da Liberdade, 165. Baixa, 164. Basilica of Estrêla, 169. Belem (*see separate entry*). Belvedere of Nossa Senhora do Monte, 166. Botanical Gardens, 169. Cais do Colunas, 163. Cais do Sodre, 164. Casa dos Bicos, 168, No. 97. Castle of St George, 162, 166, No. 101. Cathedral, 20, 26, 167, 224, No. 99. Charles Depierre Lycée, 176. Chiado (Rua Garrett), 168. *Churches*: of the Carmo, 21, 168, No. 100; Estrêla, 23; Madre Deus, 170; Nossa Senhora da Fatima, 165; Graça, 166; São Roque, 169; São Vicente de Fora, 23, 166, No. 120; Santa Engracia, 166; Santo Antonio de Sé, 167; Concecião Velha, 168. *Convents*: Madre de Deus, 27, 167; Santo Alberto, 169. Edward VII Park, 165. *Museums*: Ancient Art, 26, 96, 169-73, Nos. 113-19; Archaeological (in Carmo Convent), 168; Coach, 173-4; Military, 167; Modern Art, 28, 169; Popular Art, 175; Sacred Art, 169; Vasconceles Ethnological, 174. *Palaces*: Foz, 165; Necessidades, 173; Ajuda, 173; Belem, 173; Fronteira, No. 3. *Praça*: de D. Pedro, or Rossio, 165; do Comercio, 23, 163, 164, 166, 167; Marquès de Pombal, 165; dos Restauradores, 165, No. 98; de Touros, 165; de Camões, 168; Afonso de Albuquerque, 173; Restelo, 173; Rossio, 166. *Railway stations*: South, 164; South East, 164; Cais do Sodre, 164; Central, 165. *Rua*: Almirante Reis, 166; Augusta, 165; Garrett, 168; das Janeles Verdes, 169; Joachim Antonio de Aguiar, 176; do Ouro, 165; da Prata, 165. *Theatres*: Maria II, 165; San Carlos, 168. Travessa de São João de Parça, 168
Liz, river, 124
Loire valley, 125
Loison, 222
Lopes, Cristovão, painter, 27, 175
Lopes, Gregorio, painter, 27, 43
Lopes, Texeira, sculptor, 26, 91
Lopes Pacheco, Diogo, 16
Lorette, Francis, 94
Louis XIV, 176, 227
Louis XV, 176, 177
Loulé, 250
Lourdes, 124
Lourinha, No. 9
Lousa, Serra da, 12
Ludwig, Frederic, architect, 23, 177, 224
Luis I, 20, 49, 267
Lusitania, 14; the Lusitanians, 14, 28
Luso, 99
Luz de Lagos, 247

Mabuse, painter, 170
Machim, sculptor, 94
Madeira, 16
Madrid, 165, 170
Mafra, 23, 26, 177-8
Magalão, Ferdinand de, 17
Maia, Manuel da, engineer, 163
Malabar, 17
Malacca, 17
Malhão da Estrêla, Mont, 86
Malta, knights of, 48
Manuel, Reinaldo, architect, 23
Manuel I, 17, 22, 23, 25, 27, 50, 93, 96, 122, 127, 128, 131, 168, 170, 174, 175, 177, 222, 223, 266
Manuel II, 20, 267
Manueline art, 21-2, 25, 83, 93, 94, 95, 97, 99, 122, 123, 126, 127, 132, 167, 168, 174, 175, 177, 178, 226, 246, 249
Manuelinho, 222
Marão, Serra, 12
Maretti, mosaicist, 169

Maria I, 19, 25, 169, 174, 175, 179, 267
Maria II, 20, 267
Mariana, Queen, 177
Martires, Fr Bartolomeu dos, archbishop, 47
Masséna, Marshal, 19
Master of Celas, 96
Master of the Prodigal Son, 96
Masucci, mosaicist, 169
Mediterranean Sea, 12, 250
Melo, Francisco de, 25
Melo, Jorge de, bishop, 25, 227
Memling, Hans, painter, 170
Menendiz, Geda, goldsmith, 97
Meneses, Duarte de, 179
Meneses, Rui de, 168
Meneses family, 90
Mertola, gorges of, 13
Meseta, the, 11, 12
Methuen Treaty, 18, 49
Metsys, Quentin, painter, 27, 91, 96, 170
Michelangelo, 225
Miguel, Don (Miguel I), 20, 267
Milreu, 250
Mina, castle of, 17
Minho, province of, 12, 13, 41, 44-8
Minho, river, 11, 13, 47, 246
Miranda do Douro, 41-2, Nos. 15-16
Mirandela, 41, 42, No. 14
Moluccas, the, 17
Monchique, Serra de, 246, 247, 249, Nos. 152, 154-7
Mondego district, 15, 92
Mondego valley, 26, 82, 90, 91, 92, 95, 98, 99, 122, 131, No. 6
Monserrate, Quinta de, 177
Monteiro, Pardal, architect, 165
Montemor-o-novo, 221
Montemor-o-Velho, 90
Montemuro plateau, 42
Montes Claros promontory, 176
Montherlant, H. de, writer, 130
Montijo, 18
Moors, 14, 15, 28, 45, 163, 177, 222, 223, 225
Morais, Cristovão de, painter, 171, No. 113
Morena, Serra, 12
Morocco, 123
Moura, Isabella de, 171, No. 114
Mozambique, 20
Murça, 43-4

Murcia, 13
Muslims, 11, 14, 15, 222, 245

Napoleon, 19
Narvão, river, 121
Nazaré, 131-2, 178, Nos. 4, 83-93
Nazzoni, Nicolas, architect, 23
Nelson, Lord, 248
Nicolas, sculptor, 174
Nogueira, Serra, 12
Norwegians, 17
Nossa Senhora de Guadeloupe, 247-8
Nossa Senhora da Oliveira, abbey of (Guimarães), 44, 45
Nossa Senhora da Pena, chapel of (Leiria), 124
Nossa Senhora dos Remedios, sanctuary of (Lamego), 42
Numes Tinocco, Pedro, architect, 93
Nunes, Pedro, sculptor, 224
Nunez, Silvestre, 96

Obidos, 132
Obidos, Joseph de, painter, 225
Olhão, 250
Olivença, 19
Oporto, 13, 16, 28, 41, 49-50, 51, 82, 265, Nos. 30-5. Avenida dos Aliados, 49. Cathedral, 20, 23, 49. Convent of Santa Clara, 50. *Churches*: Carmelite, No. 35; Cedofeita, 50; dos Clerigos, 23; São Bento de Vitoria, 50; São Francisco, 50. *Bridges*: King Luis, 49, No. 31; Maria Pia, 49. Museum of Soares dos Reis, 50. Praça da Liberdade, 49. Santo Antonio hospital, 50. São Bento railway station, 49. Torre dos Clerigos, 23, 49
Orley, Bernard van, painter, 50, 96
Ougete, architect, 125-6
Ourem, heath of, 123
Ovar, 89
Oviedo mountains, 15

Pachecho, Duarte, minister, 165, 176
Pachecho, bridge of Duarte, 176
Pais, Bishop Durando, 224
Pais, Guladim, 121
Palha, Mar da (Sea of Straw), 13, 162, 164
Palladio, Andrea, architect, 123
Palmela, fortress of, 178
Paris, 164, 165

Index

Pedras Salgadas, 43
Pedro, Bishop, 45
Pedro, Infante, 17
Pedro, Mestre Frei, 130
Pedro I, Emperor, 19–20
Pedro I (Pedro the Cruel), 15–16, 24, 130–1, 265, 266, No. 81
Pedro II, 18, 267
Pedro V, 20, 267
Penacova, 99
Penafiel, 48
Penhas, Douradas, rocks of the, 86
Penicaud, Jean II, engraver, 50
Peniche, 132
Pereira, Gonzalo, archbishop, 24, 45–6
Perfect Prince, the. See John II
Périgord, 125
Peter, Regent, Duke of Coimbra, 127
Peter the Cruel. See Pedro I
Petit, Jean, 222
Philip the Good, 27
Philip II, of Spain, 18, 123, 223
Philip IV, of Spain, 18
Philippa, Queen, 16 *note*, 125, 127
Phoenicians, 14, 89, 132
Picota, La, mountain, 249
Piedade, Ponta da, 246, 247
Pillement, painter, 28, 170
Pinhão, 51
Pinheiro, Diogo, 121
Pires, Manuel, architect, 225
Pires, Marcos, architect, 22, 97
Pires the elder, Diogo, sculptor, 25
Pires-o-Moco, Diogo, sculptor, 97
Plateresque art, 22
Poblet, 131
Pombal, Marquès de, 19, 23, 163, 168, 169, 222, 250
Pontigny, 129
Portalegre, 227, No. 145
Portimão, 249
Portinho de Arrabida, 178
Povoa de Varzim, 48, No. 29
Praia da Rocha, 249, No. 159
Praia de Vieria, No. 168
Pyrenees, Peace of the, 18

Queluz, Palace of, 23, 176–7, No. 121
Quillard, painter, 28, 170

Raposeira, 248
Reconquest of Portugal, 15, 45, 250
Reis, Soares dos, sculptor, 26, 50
Resende, Garcia de, chronicler, 222
Ribatejo, province of, 13, 121, 179, No. 126
Robert, architect, 94, 167
Robillon, J. B., architect, 176
Roca, Cape, 12
Roderick, king of the Goths, 86
Rome, the Romans, 14, 20, 28, 43, 45, 83, 98, 162, 163, 166, 169, 222, 250
Rouen, Jean de, sculptor, 25–6, 84, 90, 94, 97, 98, 174
Roupinho, Fuas, 131

Saboia, 249
Sado, river, 11, 13
Sagres, Cape and promontory of, 16, 247, 248, 249, Nos. 158, 160
St James of Compostella, 47
St George of Albujarrota, chapel of, 129
St Vincent, Cape, 16, 247, 248, 249
Salado, battle of, 222
Salamanca, 82, 224
Salazar, Dr, 20; Salazar régime, 20, 165, 265
Salvatierra de Magos, 179
Salvi, architect, 169
San Martinho de Porto, 132
Sancho I, 15, 25, 42, 45, 93, 170, 266
Sancho II, 15, 266
Santa Clara, Convent of, 90
Santa Clara, Convent of (Vila do Conde), 48
Santa Luzia, church of (Viana do Castelo), 48
Santa Maria, 12
Santa Marinha da Costa, 45
Santa Tecla, 47
Santarem, 166, 178, 179
Santos, Eugénio dos, engineer, 163
Santos, Reynaldo dos, 21
São Bento de Castris, Convent of, 226
São Domingos, church of (Valença do Minho), 47
São Domingos, monastery of (Guimarães), 45
São Frutuoso, church of (Braga), 20, 46
São Marcos, monastery of, 25, 90
São Pedro do Sul, 88
São Sebastião fountain, No. 36
São Thomé, 18
São Tiago de Cacém, 228, 245

Sebastian, King, 18, 171, 175, 222, 223, 246, 266, No. 113
Segovia, 168
Sempavor, Geraldo, 222
Sequeira, Domingos, painter, 28, 171
Sesimbra, fortress of, 178, Nos. 123-4
Setubal, 12, 13, 22, 178, No. 125
Seville, 26, 170
Silva family, 90
Silves, 21, 249-50
Sintra, Serra da, 12, 177
Sintra (Pena Palace), 22, 25, 177, No. 122
Soares dos Reis. *See* Reis
Sousa, Diogo de, archbishop, 45, 46
Sousa, Gonçalo de, 168
Spain, Spanish domination, 11, 14, 18, 19, 24, 27, 41, 82, 83, 125, 130, 165, 170, 173, 222, 226, 248
Straw, Sea of (Mar da Palha), 13, 162, 164
Suevians, 28

Tagus, river, 11, 13, 15, 162, 163, 164, 174, 177, 178, 179, 221, Nos. 2, 10
Tangier, 17
Tarragona, 131
Tavira, 250, No. 161
Templars, the, 21, 48, 121, 122
Teresa of Avila, St, 85
Terzi, Filippo, architect, 23, 95, 123, 166, 169
Tibães, monastery of (Braga), 46
Tinoccos, the, architects, 23
Toledo, 15, 26
Tomar, 22, 99, 121-3, Nos. 62-8. *Churches*: Santa Iria, 121; São João Baptista, 122; Santa Maria de Conceição, 23, 123; Santa Maria do Olival 121. *Cloisters*: of the Cemetery, 123; of Felipes, 94, 123; of the guest quarters, 123; of Santa Barbara, 123. Monastery (Convent of Christ), 22, 23, 122, 126, 174, Nos. 62-8. San Tiago gate, 122
Tordesillas, 17
Torralva, Diogo de, 23, 123, 174, 225
Torres Vedras, 19
Tourville, 248
Trás-os-Montes, province of, 12, 13, 41-4, 50, No. 12
Travanca, 48-9
Turks, 16
Turrianos, the, architects, 23

Tuscany, 121
Tuy, 47
Utrecht, Cristovão of, painter, 43 *note*

Valença do Minho, 13, 47
Valladolid, 82
Vallejo, Felipe de, goldsmith, 226
Valois, Marguerite de, 50
Vanvitelli, architect, 169
Varziela, 26, 90
Vasco, the Great. *See* Fernandes, Vasco
Vasques, Martin, architect, 126
Vauban, engineer, 223
Vaz, Pero and Gaspar, painters, 88
Velazquez, painter, 27
Velho, Tomé, sculptor, 95
Venice, 17, 47
Verde, Cape, 16
Versailles, 176
Viana do Costelo, 13, 47-8, Nos. 26-7
Vicente, Gil, goldsmith, 170, 222
Vicente, Mateus, 23, 176
Vicente de Almeida, José and Felix, sculptors, 173
Vidago, 43
Vieira, Domingos, painter, 171, No. 114
Vila do Bispo, 248
Vila do Conde, 23
Vila Franca de Xira, 166, 178, 179, Nos. 94, 126-34
Vila Nova de Familição, No. 38
Vila Nova da Gaia, 49, 51
Vila Real, 41, 42, 44
Vila Real de San Antonio, 250, Nos. 162-3
Vila Vicosa, 226
Vilar Formoso, 83
Vincent, St, 26, 248
Viriathus, 14, 86
Viseu, 27, 43, 82, 85, 86-8, Nos. 10, 42
Visigoths, 28, 163, 222
Vista Alegre, 90
Vouga, river, 12, 14, 88

Watteau, Antoine, painter, 170
Wellington, Duke of, 19
West Indies, 17

York Cathedral, 126

Zamora, 224
Zurbaran, painter, 170